SECOND EDITION

COMMUNICATING
iN BUSINESS
ENGLISH

1

Content

How to Use

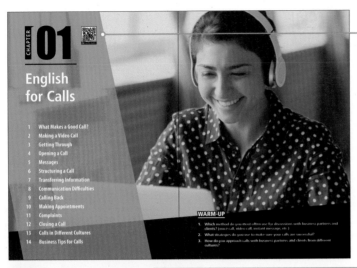

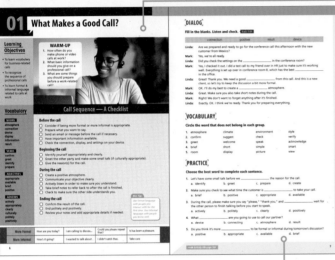

Lessons

The first page of every lesson gives lesson objectives, topical warm-up questions, target vocabulary, and useful language or functional information.

The second page of each lesson provides a topic-relevant listening and vocabulary exercises.

Activities

Every lesson has an additional practice activity in the Activity File section at the back of the book to actively reinforce learned vocabulary, structures, and situational strategies. Scan the QR code at the start of the Activity File for activity audio.

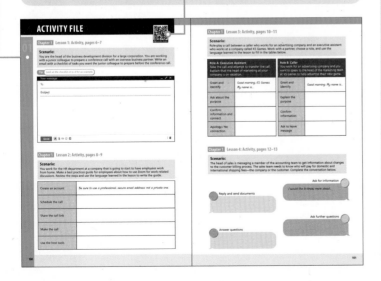

Study Booster

Every lesson has further practice exercises on our digital platform.

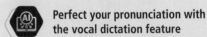 Improve your conversation skills with authentic dialogs

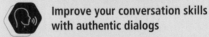 Perfect your pronunciation with the vocal dictation feature

 Build your vocabulary with the extensive word library

CHAPTER 01

Scan for Audio

English for Calls

WARM-UP

1. Which method do you most often use for discussions with business partners and clients? (voice call, video call, instant message, etc.)

2. What strategies do you use to make sure your calls are successful?

3. How do you approach calls with business partners and clients from different cultures?

01 What Makes a Good Call?

Learning Objectives

- To learn vocabulary for business-related calls
- To recognize the sequence of professional calls
- To learn formal & informal language related to calls at work

WARM-UP

1. How often do you make phone or video calls at work?
2. What basic information should you give on a professional call?
3. What are some things you should prepare before a work-related call?

Vocabulary

NOUNS
atmosphere
connection
device
display
information
result

VERBS
confirm
greet
identify
prepare

ADJECTIVES
appropriate
available
brief
positive

ADVERBS
actively
appropriately
clearly
culturally
politely
positively

Call Sequence — A Checklist

Before the call
- ☐ Consider if being more formal or more informal is appropriate.
- ☐ Prepare what you want to say.
- ☐ Send an email or message before the call if necessary.
- ☐ Have important information available.
- ☐ Check the connection, display, and settings on your device.

Beginning the call
- ☐ Identify yourself appropriately and clearly.
- ☐ Greet the other party and make some small talk (if culturally appropriate).
- ☐ Give the reason(s) for the call.

During the call
- ☐ Create a positive atmosphere.
- ☐ Communicate your objective clearly.
- ☐ Actively listen in order to make sure you understand.
- ☐ Take brief notes to refer back to after the call is finished.
- ☐ Check to make sure the other side understands you.

Ending the call
- ☐ Confirm the result of the call.
- ☐ End politely and positively.
- ☐ Review your notes and add appropriate details if needed.

Biz Tip

Use formal language with people you interact with for the first time. Use informal language with people you know well.

More Formal	How are you today?	I am calling to discuss...	Could you please repeat that?	It has been a pleasure.
More Informal	How's it going?	I wanted to talk about...	I didn't catch that.	Take care.

DIALOG

Fill in the blanks. Listen and check. Track 1-01

connection	positive	result	device

Linda: Are we prepared and ready to go for the conference call this afternoon with the new customer from Mexico?

Mark: Yes, we're all ready.

Linda: Did you check the settings on the _____ in the conference room?

Mark: Yes, I checked it out. I did a test call to my friend over in HR just to make sure it's working well. Everything is set up over in conference room B, which has the best _____ in the office.

Linda: Great! Thank you. We need a good _____ from this call. And this is a new client, so let's try to keep the discussion a bit more formal.

Mark: OK. I'll do my best to create a _____ atmosphere.

Linda: Great. Make sure you also take short notes during the call.

Mark: Right! We don't want to forget anything after it's finished.

Linda: Exactly. OK. I think we're ready. Thank you for preparing everything.

VOCABULARY

Circle the word that does not belong in each group.

1.	atmosphere	climate	environment	style
2.	confirm	suggest	check	verify
3.	greet	welcome	speak	acknowledge
4.	brief	short	simple	smart
5.	room	display	picture	view

PRACTICE

Choose the best word to complete each sentence.

1. Let's have some small talk before we _____ the reason for the call.
   a. identify   b. greet   c. prepare   d. create

2. Make sure you check to see what time the customer is _____ to take your call.
   a. brief   b. positive   c. appropriate   d. available

3. During the call, please make sure you say "please," "thank you," and _____ wait for the other person to finish talking before you start to speak.
   a. actively   b. politely   c. clearly   d. positively

4. What _____ are you going to use to call our partner?
   a. device   b. connecting   c. atmosphere   d. result

5. Do you think it's more _____ to be formal or informal during tomorrow's discussion?
   a. positive   b. appropriate   c. available   d. brief

02 Making a Video Call

Learning Objectives

- To learn vocabulary for video calls
- To understand best practices for making and receiving video calls
- To practice prepositions related to calls at work

WARM-UP

1. What devices and tools do you need to make a video call for work?
2. How should you prepare for a work-related call?
3. Have you ever used Skype, Zoom, or another piece of software for professional online calls?

Vocabulary

NOUNS
account
availability
chat
contact
host
invitation
link
participant
program
tool

VERBS
activate
admit
create
join
launch
mute
schedule

ADJECTIVES
secure

ADVERBS
promptly
properly

Making a Video Call — Dos & Don'ts

		Do	Don't
Create an account		use a professional and secure email address	use a personal or a private email address
		activate the account right away	wait to activate the account
Schedule the call		use a group chat	email the participants separately
		confirm the availability of the participants	wait too long to hear back from the participants
Share the call link		create an invitation link and share it before the call	create an invitation link just before the call starts
		click the link to make sure it works properly	share the link without testing it first
Make the call		launch the calling program a few minutes early and wait for people to join	launch the calling program exactly on time
		admit the participants promptly	keep the participants waiting
Use the host tools		mute yourself and others while listening	allow the call to get too noisy
		send files and messages as needed	send unnecessary files or messages

Preposition	on...	in...	via...
Meaning	using (communications that transmit information)	at a particular place that we can see	by way of
Examples	Find it **on** the internet. I am **on** the phone.	Type it **in** the chat. It is **in** the agenda.	Have a call **via** Zoom. Send it **via** email.

DIALOG

Fill in the blanks. Listen and check. `Track 1-02`

tools	participants	account	via

Greg: Hello, this is Greg in Human Resources. Who is calling, please?

Linda: Hi, Greg, this is Linda from the Management team. Were you able to create that Zoom _____?

Greg: Oh, hi, Linda. Yes, I activated it yesterday.

Linda: Great. Thank you. Did you have a chance to use it and get familiar with the _____ in the program?

Greg: Yes, I checked it out a little bit, and I think it is fairly easy to use.

Linda: Wonderful. Actually, we need to schedule a call for next week with our HQ in San Diego. I would like to do it _____ Zoom if possible.

Greg: OK. Sure. I can do that. Can you send me a list of contacts who will participate in the call via email? I need to check the availability of the _____ in advance.

Linda: No problem. I can send that to you after lunch.

Greg: Perfect! After I have confirmed everyone's availability, I will create a link and share it on the company message board.

VOCABULARY

Match the words that have the same meaning.

1. admit •   • a. start
2. launch •   • b. let in
3. create •   • c. on time
4. promptly •   • d. safe
5. secure •   • e. make

PRACTICE

Fill in the blanks with the correct word.

properly	mute	invitation	join	chat

1. I can't hear you that well because I think your mic isn't working _____.

2. Use the _____ feature while other people are talking so you can communicate politely.

3. Try to _____ the call a few minutes early.

4. I sent you the _____ via email. Did you get it?

5. It is polite to _____ your mic when you aren't speaking, so as not to accidentally interrupt the other participants.

03 Getting Through

Learning Objectives

- To learn vocabulary for directing phone calls
- To understand a range of phrases for transferring calls
- To practice phrasal verbs related to calls at work

WARM-UP

1. What is a polite way to answer the phone at work when you don't know who is calling?
2. How do you politely introduce yourself on a work call when a stranger answers?
3. What are some other good habits when on a work-related call with an unfamiliar person?

Vocabulary

NOUNS
behalf
confirmation
customer
menu
representative

VERBS
apologize
assist
connect
deliver
hang up
hold
reach
regard
take down
transfer

ADJECTIVES
afraid
automated
out
urgent

ADVERBS
slowly

Transferring Calls — A Process

Greet and identify your company / department
- Good morning. Lake Technology.
- I'm a customer service representative, and my name is Jessica.

Ask about the purpose
- How can I assist you?
- What is your call in regard to?

Identify the caller and confirm their information
- I apologize, but could you spell your name for me?
- Thank you. And could I have your phone number in case we get disconnected?

Connection
- Please hold while I get confirmation on that for you.
- One moment, please, while I try to reach him / her.

Apologies and no connections
- I am sorry, but I am afraid...
  → he / she is out sick today.
  → he / she is out on business.
- Could I take down and deliver a message for you?
- Sorry, could you say that once more a bit more slowly?

Make the connection
- Please hold while I transfer your call.
- One moment, please, while I connect you.

Biz Tip

Use verbs in a more serious, formal situation, and phrasal verbs when you want to create a more friendly, slightly less serious atmosphere.

Verb	record	assist	connect	end
Phrasal Verb	take down	help out	get / put through	hang up

DIALOG

Fill in the blanks. Listen and check. Track 1-03

behalf	assist	representative	take down

Jessica: Good morning. Lake Technology. I'm a customer service _____, and my name is Jessica. How may I assist you today?

Calvin: Hello, Jessica. My name is Calvin. I'm calling on _____ of Future Capital. Our company is looking to set up a new software security system.

Jessica: Hello, Calvin. We can certainly help you with that. I'll need to transfer you to Mr. Barratt, who is in charge of B2B sales. He can further _____ you with your needs. Could you hold while I see if he is available?

Calvin: Yes.

Jessica: Thank you. One moment, please. Hello, Calvin. I do apologize, but it seems that Mr. Barratt is out on vacation until next week. Could we _____ your contact information and deliver a message for Mr. Barratt to contact you as soon as he returns?

Calvin: Sure. That would be great!

Jessica: Thank you. We have an automated system for that. I will transfer you, and you can use the menu to leave a message and enter your contact information for Mr. Barratt.

Calvin: Thank you!

VOCABULARY

Complete each definition with a word from the vocabulary list.

1. When you are sorry about something, you can _____.

2. When you are finished with a phone call, you _____.

3. Before transferring you to an actual person, many companies have an _____ system.

4. If something needs to be done right away, then it is _____.

5. If someone is not available to take a call, you can say they are _____.

PRACTICE

Match each question with the correct response.

1. How can I assist you today?
    •
    • a. Please tell her it's urgent and to call me back ASAP.

2. I apologize, but could you spell your name for me? •
    • b. I'm trying to reach Mr. Barratt.

3. Could I have your contact information? •
    • c. Yes, I'll send it to you via email.

4. Would you like me to deliver a message to her on your behalf? •
    • d. Sure. It's Hong. That's H-O-N-G.

5. Could you hold while I see if he's available? •
    • e. Absolutely.

04 Opening a Call

Learning Objectives

- To learn vocabulary for opening a work call
- To respond to information shared before a call
- To learn common work-related abbreviations

WARM-UP

1. What are the most common reasons you make calls at work?
2. How often do you make contact via messenger before a call?
3. What kind of information is useful to share before a work-related call?

Vocabulary

NOUNS
billing
details
fee
inquiry
invoice
message
messenger
notice

VERBS
discuss
receive
reference
simplify
text / message
depend on

ADJECTIVES
advance
complicated
detailed
technical
tedious
unclear

Opening a Call — A Checklist

Sending messages before the call

- ☐ Send important information that will help the other person prepare.
- ☐ Send information that they may need to reference before or after the call.
- ☐ Send complicated, detailed, technical, and tedious information.

Beginning the call

- ☐ Identify yourself appropriately and clearly.
- ☐ Greet the other party and make some small talk (if culturally appropriate).
- ☐ Give the reason(s) for the call.

Referring to information shared before the call

- ☐ Confirm that shared information was received.
- ☐ Confirm that shared information was understood.
- ☐ Discuss any points that are unclear.

Proceeding with the call

- ☐ Clearly move to the next agenda item for the call.
- ☐ Share additional information, files, etc. via messenger during the call if necessary.
- ☐ State any information that will be shared via messenger after the call is finished.

> **Biz Tip**
>
> *Abbreviations are more common in written communication than in spoken communication, and are more appropriate in more informal situations.*

Abbreviation	FYI	IMO	e.g.	i.e.	doc
Meaning	For your information,	In my opinion,	For example,	In other words,	document

DIALOG

Fill in the blanks. Listen and check. `Track 1-04`

inquiries	advance	simplify	FYI

Marty: How are things on your end?

Lani: Yeah, can't complain. By the way, did you receive the message I sent to you yesterday evening in preparation for this call?

Marty: Yes, I did. Thank you for the _____ notice of the new billing process. It was really helpful to support our staff's understanding of the new system.

Lani: Absolutely! The new process is supposed to _____ things a bit, but in my opinion, it still seems to be a little complicated.

Marty: Yeah, now that you mention it, some of my staff sent me a few _____. In particular, for international invoices over $500, who is meant to pay the wire transfer fee?

Lani: I'll send you a doc with all of that information because it actually depends on the country. I'll text that over right now. Just a moment. OK, did you get it?

Marty: Yes, I got it. Thank you. By the way, just _____, I'll be out of the office tomorrow, so I'll message you the other questions tonight on my way home from the office.

Lani: Great. I'll watch out for those and get back to you ASAP.

VOCABULARY

Choose the best word or phrase to match the meaning of the underlined words.

1. The new policy on communicating is a little <u>confusing</u>.
   a. unclear   b. technical   c. detailed   d. advanced

2. Could you <u>send</u> that information over to me ASAP?
   a. receive   b. simplify   c. text   d. discuss

3. What is the call <u>about</u>?
   a. inquiry   b. message   c. details   d. regarding

4. You can <u>look at</u> the information I sent before the call.
   a. invoice   b. reference   c. depend on   d. notice

5. The billing <u>is decided by</u> the size of the order.
   a. tedious   b. invoice   c. receive   d. depends on

PRACTICE

Fill in the blank with the correct abbreviation from the abbreviation guide.

1. _____, I'll be in a meeting all morning before our call this afternoon.

2. The new system is better than the previous one, _____.

3. We need to get this done very quickly, _____, it should have been done yesterday.

4. The _____ you sent with advance notice was helpful.

5. We need more details about shipping, _____, the weight limits per container.

05 Messages

Learning Objectives

- To learn vocabulary for giving and receiving contact details
- To understand the process for delivering messages
- To practice language for confirming understanding

WARM-UP

1. How often do you leave or receive messages at work?
2. What information do you need to give when leaving a message?
3. What information do you need to get when receiving a message?

Vocabulary

NOUNS
action
address
area code
date

VERBS
affirm
call back
go ahead
inform
make sure
proceed
provide
repeat
reschedule
reply
return
spell
tell

ADJECTIVES
corporate
correct

PREPOSITION
except

Leaving & Receiving Messages — A Process

Names and addresses

- Could I have your name again, please?
- Could you provide me with the street address?

Contact details

- How would you like to be contacted?
- What is your email address / phone number?

The message

- Please inform him / her that I called and ask him / her to reply.
- Could you ask him / her to return my call ASAP?

Checking spelling

- Could you spell your / that name for me, please?
- My name is Sharon. That's S-H-A-R-O-N.
- Could you repeat the spelling for me one more time?

Reassuring action

- I'll make sure he / she gets your message.
- I will have him / her contact you as soon as he / she comes back to the office.
- I'll proceed to get this message to him / her right away.

Thanking

- Thank you for providing that information.
- I appreciate you delivering the message on my behalf.

> **Biz Tip**
>
> Ask people taking information "Would you like me to spell that for you?" to prevent miscommunication.

Spelling Things	A = Apple	B = Boy	C = Cat	D = Door	E = Egg	F = Farm	G = Girl
	H = Hair	I = Igloo	J = Jar	K = Kite	L = Lost	M = Mom	N = North
	O = Ox	P = Pan	Q = Queen	R = Ram	S = Sun	T = Top	U = Umbrella
	V = Vest	W = Word	X = X-Ray	Y = Yarn	Z = Zebra	= "as in" when speaking	

DIALOG

Fill in the blanks. Listen and check. `Track 1-05`

reschedule	corporate	O as in Ox	inform

Hunter: Lori is out on vacation at the moment. Could I take a message for you?

Sharon: My name is Sharon. I'm supposed to have a lunch meeting with Lori next week, but I need to _____.

Hunter: I see. One moment, please. Let me take down your information and a message. OK, and do you spell your name S-H-A-R-E-N?

Sharon: Yes, that's correct except for the "E." It's actually an _____. S-H-A-R-O-N.

Hunter: Thank you. And you want to reschedule your lunch meeting to which date?

Sharon: I'd like to move it to the 30th of this month. I want to confirm if that works for Lori.

Hunter: Alright. I will _____ her about that and ask her to return your call. Could you provide your contact details, please?

Sharon: Yes, please ask her to call me back on my _____ phone. The number is 412-0730.

Hunter: Alright. And just to make sure, the area code is 318, right?

Sharon: Yes, that is correct.

Hunter: Thank you very much. I'll tell Lori to return your call as soon as possible.

VOCABULARY

Fill in the blanks in the following message using the words below.

Address	reschedule	Action	return	Date

1. _____: July 30th

2. _____: 8385 Metro Building

3. Message: Wants to _____ meeting

4. _____: Please _____ phone call ASAP.

PRACTICE

Put the following sentences in logical order (a = first, e = last).

1. _____ Hello, how can I assist you today?

2. _____ And just to make sure, could you let me know the area code, please?

3. _____ Could I have your contact information, please?

4. _____ Thank you, I will make sure she calls you back soon.

5. _____ I'm sorry, she is out sick today. Can I take a message?

Learning Objectives

- To learn vocabulary for different parts of business-related calls
- To recognize how to structure professional calls
- To learn language to delay topics

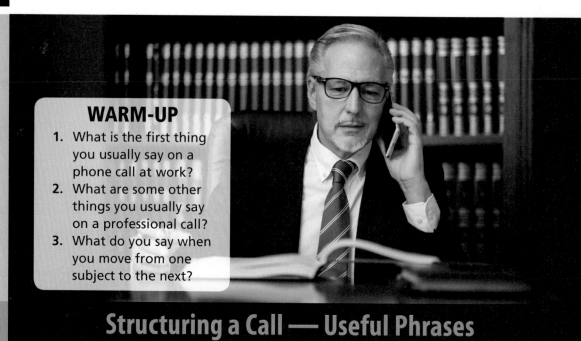

WARM-UP

1. What is the first thing you usually say on a phone call at work?
2. What are some other things you usually say on a professional call?
3. What do you say when you move from one subject to the next?

Vocabulary

NOUNS

agreement
logistics
purpose

VERBS

arrange
assign
check
deal with
delay
explain
follow up
get back to
handle
leave to
organize
structure

ADJECTIVES

acceptable

ADVERBS

carefully
finally
first
second

Structuring a Call — Useful Phrases

Stating the purpose

- I am calling to arrange / discuss / explain / organize...
- I would like to deal with / inquire about...

Structuring

- There are three things I would like to talk about.
- First, / Second, / Finally, I'd like to discuss...

Checking

- Is that OK with you?
- Would this be acceptable?
- Are you in agreement with that?

Assigning

- Should I deal with the logistics?
- I need you to handle...

Delaying

- Can we put that off until...?
- I will have to get back to you about...

Setting action items

- Could you send me an email to follow up on that?
- I will inform him / her after this call.

Confirming

- Is there anything else?
- I think that's about it, right?

> **Biz Tip**
>
> The structure of a call doesn't always follow the same sequence from start to finish, so be prepared to adapt.

Expressions to Delay a Topic	Let's put a pin in that until...	Can we circle back to that when...?	Could we table that until...?	Could we return to that after...?

DIALOG

Fill in the blanks. Listen and check. Track 1-06

leave it to	arrange	put a pin in that	follow up

Linda: I'm calling to confirm that we received your order. However, we need to _____ a billing schedule for that.

Frank: Would it be alright if we _____ until the manager of our accounting team returns from vacation? I don't usually deal with payment schedules.

Linda: Alright, no problem. Should I call back at a later date or leave a message?

Frank: The accounting team manager will be back on the 18th. I have your contact details, and I know what this is regarding, so I think you can _____ me to inform her about it.

Linda: Great! Thank you. Then I will let you handle it.

Frank: Alright. Is there anything else you wanted to discuss?

Linda: Not really. But could you _____ with me about this by the 20th? I need to enter the billing schedule for your order into our system by that date.

Frank: Understood. We'll deal with this first thing when she returns.

VOCABULARY

Match the words that have the same meaning.

1. purpose •
2. agreement •
3. delay •
4. handle •
5. explain •

• a. understanding
• b. tell
• c. take care of
• d. reason
• e. wait

PRACTICE

Write the phrase to describe the function of each sentence.

stating the purpose	structuring	delaying	confirming	setting action items

1. "There are two things I'd like to talk about today." _____

2. "I'm calling to confirm that we received your order." _____

3. "Could you follow up with me about this by the 20th?" _____

4. "Is there anything else you wanted to discuss?" _____

5. "Could we put a pin in that until my manager returns?" _____

Learning Objectives

- To learn vocabulary for transferring information
- To practice active listening skills
- To learn language related to confirming information

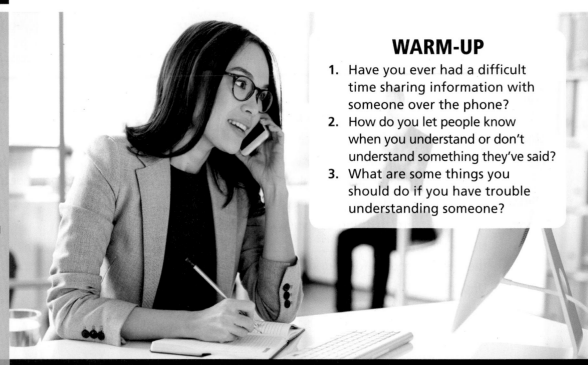

WARM-UP

1. Have you ever had a difficult time sharing information with someone over the phone?
2. How do you let people know when you understand or don't understand something they've said?
3. What are some things you should do if you have trouble understanding someone?

Vocabulary

NOUNS

miscommunication
mistake

VERBS

break up
cancel
catch
excuse
follow
go over
go through
mean
pardon
read back
respond
state

ADJECTIVES

accurate
critical

ADVERBS

exactly
precisely
quite

Transferring Information — Useful Phrases

Starting

- Do you have something to take this information down with?
- Are you ready to write this down?

Signaling understanding

- OK. / Uh-huh.
- Yes. / Right.
- Got it.

Signaling misunderstanding

- Sorry? I didn't quite catch that. Could you state it once more?
- Pardon me, but the connection seems to be breaking up.
- Excuse me, but I don't follow. Could you please go over that again?

Signaling a mistake

- Sorry, I think that's a mistake. It should be...
- That's not quite accurate. What I mean is...
- Sorry, not the 30th. I said the 13th, as in one-three.

Checking

- Did you get all of that?
- Should I repeat / spell that?
- Could you read that back to me, please?
- So you want that to be canceled?

Phrases for Confirming	Let me read it back to you.	Yes, you said...	OK. Let's go through that once more. First,...

DIALOG

Fill in the blanks. Listen and check. `Track 1-07`

miscommunication	exactly	read this back	Pardon

Beth: Could you give Chris a message for me when he gets in? Are you ready?

Alan: Uh-huh. Go ahead, please.

Beth: A VIP named Ms. Yoon is flying in tonight. We need someone to meet her at the airport, but I'm going to be on a conference call with an international business partner.

Alan: OK. Could you spell her name for me?

Beth: Yes, it's Y-O-O-N. She's arriving on the 7:50 flight from San Francisco.

Alan: Sorry? I didn't quite catch the time. Did you say 7:15?

Beth: _____ me. Not 15, but 50, as in five-zero. It's critical we don't keep her waiting at the airport, so ask Chris to be there promptly.

Alan: Right. And just to make sure there's no _____, I will _____ to you. Chris should be at the airport to pick up a VIP flying in from San Francisco. Her name is Ms. Yoon, that's Y-O-O-N, and he needs to be there before 7:50. Did I get all that?

Beth: Yes, _____. Thank you.

VOCABULARY

Find and write a word from the vocabulary list that has the same meaning as the underlined word.

1. Sorry, I didn't <u>hear</u> that.   _____

2. I don't <u>understand</u>.   _____

3. She will <u>reply</u> as soon as possible.   _____

4. Is that information <u>correct</u>?   _____

5. It is <u>important</u> you deliver this message.   _____

PRACTICE

Match each question with the correct response.

1. Did you say 7:15?   •   • a. Yes. Please go ahead.

2. Sorry, could you spell her name for me? •   • b. Yes, it's A-N-G-I-E.

3. Sorry? I didn't quite catch that. Could   •   • c. Yes, precisely. Thanks.
   you repeat that, please?

4. Did I get all that?   •   • d. No. I said 7:50, as in five-zero.

5. Are you ready?   •   • e. Yes. I said Wednesday.

08 Communication Difficulties

Learning Objectives

- To learn vocabulary for communication issues
- To recognize how to deal with technical difficulties
- To learn expressions to solve problems with calls at work

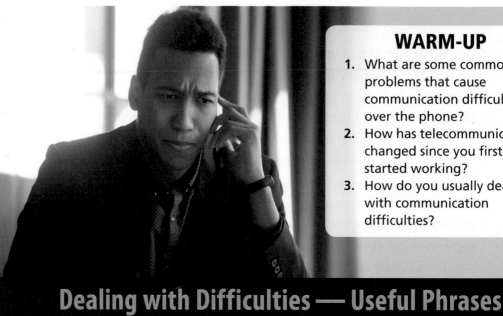

WARM-UP

1. What are some common problems that cause communication difficulties over the phone?
2. How has telecommunication changed since you first started working?
3. How do you usually deal with communication difficulties?

Vocabulary

NOUNS

answer
battery
line
problem
signal

VERBS

cut off
cut out
die
get a hold of
lose
speak up

ADJECTIVES

in service
noisy
poor
terrible
wrong

ADVERBS

back
hardly
right
suddenly

Dealing with Difficulties — Useful Phrases

Identify the problem

General problems

- There's no answer.
- He / She is on the other line with someone else.

Device problems

- The number is no longer in service.
- The battery died.

Network problems

- The signal is really poor.
- The connection is terrible.
- We suddenly got cut off.

Sound problems

- You keep cutting out.
- I can hardly hear you.
- It is very noisy.

Wrong numbers

- I'm sorry, I think you have the wrong number.
- What number are you trying to get a hold of?

Call back

- Sorry. Can I call you right back?
- In case I lose you, I will call you back.

> **Biz Tip**
>
> *You should always test your device, connection, and have solutions prepared for any potential difficulties before making an important call.*

Problem	general	device	network	sound
Phrases for Solutions	I'll try again later.	I'll use another phone.	I will text / email you.	Can you hear me now?

DIALOG

Fill in the blanks. Listen and check. `Track 1-08`

battery	hardly	wrong	hear me now

James: Hi, Tammy? I've been trying to get a hold of you all morning, but there's been no answer.

Tammy: Hello? Can you speak up? I can _____ hear you. Who is calling, please?

James: It's James! Can you _____?

Tammy: Hi, James. What's wrong? You keep cutting out. Is your _____ dying or something?

James: It's not my phone. This signal is terrible. Let me call you right back.

Tammy: Hello?

James: Hi, Tammy. It's me, James, again. The signal seems better. Can you hear me OK?

Woman: There's no Tammy here. I think you have the _____ number.

VOCABULARY

Circle the word that does not belong in each group.

1. answer	reply	response	signal
2. speak up	die	lose	cut out
3. get a hold of	speak to	line	reach
4. right	poor	wrong	terrible
5. in service	active	available	noisy

PRACTICE

Choose the best word to complete each sentence.

1. I've been calling you all day but there's been no _____.

   a. battery   b. answer   c. line   d. noisy

2. I can hardly hear you. Can you please _____?

   a. speak up   b. noisy   c. answer   d. get a hold of

3. I can hardly hear you. You keep _____.

   a. wrong   b. dying   c. losing   d. cutting out

4. This signal is _____.

   a. hardly   b. wrong   c. terrible   d. problem

5. I'm trying to _____ of Tammy. Is she there?

   a. get a hold   b. cut out   c. speak up   d. in service

→ *Activity File* page 103

09 Calling Back

Learning Objectives

- To learn vocabulary for calling people back
- To use a range of phrases for returning calls
- To practice offering to call another person back

WARM-UP

1. How often do you ask people to call back?
2. Why do you usually ask someone to call back?
3. What are some things you should say when you return a call at work?

Vocabulary

NOUNS

appointment
assistant
colleague
excuse
exhibition
journey
reason
respect
subject
talk
trip

VERBS

arrive
deny
get back
get in
offer
request

ADJECTIVES

agreeable
brief

ADVERBS

actually

Calling Back — Useful Phrases

Offering / Requesting a callback

- Can I call you back once I arrive at...?
- Could you call me back when you get in?
- What would be an agreeable time for us to reconnect?

Insisting

- Please, I'll be very brief.
- Sorry, but it's very urgent.

Offering a reason or an excuse

- Actually, I have an appointment.
- I just got back from a business trip.
- I'm busy right now.

Calling back

- My assistant said you tried to contact me.
- I received a message from my colleague that you called.
- I got your message, so I'm returning your call.

Thanking

- Thank you for letting me get back to you.
- Thank you for calling me back so soon.
- Thank you for understanding.

> **Biz Tip**
>
> Americans say "call you" while British people say "ring you" or "phone you."

Returning to a previous subject

- With respect to what we were discussing last time we talked...
- Do you remember our talk last time?

Offer to Call Back	Is now a bad time?	Should we talk again later?	Would another time be better?

DIALOG

Fill in the blanks. Listen and check. `Track 1-09`

assistant	journey	another time	actually

Seth: Hi, Marie? This is Seth. I got a message from my _____ that you called, so I'm returning your call.

Marie: Right. Hi, Seth. Yes, that's right. I called yesterday. Thanks for returning my call. I'm _____ at the airport right now though. I'm about to get on a long flight to London. We have a three-day-long exhibition this weekend.

Seth: I see. Would _____ be better?

Marie: Yes, can I call you back after I arrive at the expo and get set up?

Seth: Sure. When would be an agreeable time and date?

Marie: Let's say Friday evening. How about 6 p.m. Pacific Time?

Seth: Alright, that works for me. Talk to you then. Have a safe _____!

Marie: Thanks, Seth. Talk to you soon. Bye.

VOCABULARY

Match the words that have the same meaning.

1. colleague •
2. talk •
3. request •
4. brief •
5. offer •

• a. discussion
• b. ask
• c. short
• d. coworker
• e. give

PRACTICE

Write the phrase to describe the function of each sentence.

offering an excuse	calling back	offering / requesting a callback	thanking	insisting

1. "Actually, it's urgent." _____

2. "I'm busy." _____

3. "I got a message from my assistant that you called." _____

4. "Thanks for returning my call." _____

5. "Would another time be better?" _____

Learning Objectives

- To learn vocabulary for making appointments
- To practice various phrases related to accepting and rejecting arrangements
- To recognize appropriate prepositions of time for scheduling

WARM-UP

1. How do you prefer to make appointments?
2. When is it better to make appointments over the phone?
3. What information do you need to exchange to make an appointment?

Vocabulary

NOUNS

calendar
lobby
location
reception
reservation

VERBS

change
come up
expect
postpone
push
move up
set
sound

ADJECTIVES

convenient
free
ideal
suitable

ADVERBS

indefinitely
instead
sharp

Making Appointments — Useful Phrases

Setting a time

- When is an ideal time for you?
- Are you free on…?
- … is (most / more) convenient for me.

Setting a location

- Let's meet in the lobby of the hotel near the reception desk.
- Is an online meeting suitable for you?
- How does that new vegan restaurant sound for the client's dinner?

Setting important details

- You can expect someone to pick you up from the airport.
- I've got something else on my calendar right after our lunch.
- Can you be there at three o'clock sharp?

Changing the schedule

- Let's push the earnings call to Friday.
- Could we possibly move the presentation up to this week instead of next week?

Canceling

- The exhibition was postponed indefinitely.
- I'm so sorry, but something has suddenly come up, and we're going to need to cancel the dinner reservation.

> **Biz Tip**
>
> It is polite to apologize and offer an explanation if you need to change a schedule.

Prepositions of Time	in a minute / day / etc. in 2 weeks / 7 years / etc.	at 10:30 a.m. / noon / etc. at the end of the meeting	on Saturday / the 30th on New Year's Day
Meaning	after a minute / day / 2 weeks / 7 years / etc.	during a precise or specific time of day	referring to a specific day or date

DIALOG

Fill in the blanks. Listen and check. `Track 1-10`

in a few	reservation	come up	ideal

Matt: I do apologize, but something urgent has _____, and we're going to need to push our lunch appointment until later in the day.

Abdul: I see. My schedule for the rest of the day is full until the evening, so I'm not free again until after 5 p.m.

Matt: Oh. Well, would you like me to just change the lunch _____ to dinner at the same location, then?

Abdul: Yes, I think that's probably the most _____ time for me.

Matt: Alright. Then I will call the restaurant to change the reservation time. Can we meet in the hotel lobby around 6 p.m.?

Abdul: Yes.

Matt: OK. I will text you after confirming the reservation with the restaurant.

Abdul: Thank you. Then I'll see you _____ hours. Bye.

VOCABULARY

Match each word with the correct meaning.

1. postpone •   • a. having no exact limit

2. suitable •   • b. good for a certain use or purpose

3. sharp •   • c. exactly

4. indefinitely •   • d. a position, place, or site which is used for a specific purpose

5. location •   • e. put off to a later time

PRACTICE

Fill in the blanks of the following calendar.

reception	move up	free	change	set

October				
1	**2**	**3**	**4**	**5**
_____ conference call from 3 p.m. to 11 a.m.	call Greg and _____ meeting from today to next week	email sales team to _____ a date for the presentation	call hotel _____ to make a reservation	clear schedule to make afternoon _____

11 Complaints

Learning Objectives

- To learn vocabulary for making complaints
- To understand language related to taking a complaint
- To practice a range of phrases related to handling complaints

Vocabulary

NOUNS

complaint
error
fault
responsibility
inconvenience
manual
oversight
quality

VERBS

accept
assure
attend to
blame
damage
do about
promise
repair

ADJECTIVES

clerical

ADVERBS

as ... as possible
immediately

PREPOSITION

upon

Taking & Handling Complaints — Useful Phrases

Taking the complaint

Identifying the problem

- Excuse me, but there was damage upon delivery...
- It's now... days / weeks late.

Requesting action

- Could you please attend to this as soon as possible?
- If it isn't repaired immediately, we will have to...
- Can you do something about it?

Accepting action / Rejecting action

- OK. That's fine. / I'm sorry, but we are not able to...
- OK. That will work. / I'm afraid we can't...

Handling the complaint

Asking for information

- Could you explain exactly what the issue with the quality is?

Explaining the reason for a problem and saying sorry

- It seems there was a clerical error / oversight.
- I apologize for any inconvenience caused. I promise we will fix this.

Assigning fault and promising action

- We accept full responsibility. We should have...
- I'll deal with it / attend to it / send an engineer immediately.

> **Biz Tip**
>
> *Use the passive voice to complain in a polite way, as it focuses on the problem instead of the person.*

Active Voice	You need to **fix** it.	You should **handle** that.	You **made** a mistake.
Passive Voice	It needs to **be fixed**.	That should be **handled**.	A mistake **was made**.

DIALOG

Fill in the blanks. Listen and check. `Track 1-11`

| as soon as possible | was made | clerical | complaint |

Fely: Hello, this is Fely with MBY Incorporated. I'm calling to make a complaint. I believe a mistake _____ with an order we made.

Jose: OK. Could you explain exactly what the problem is, please?

Fely: I'm calling because we ordered a shipment of steel over two months ago, but we still haven't received it. We called once before and made a _____. We were told that the shipment would be delivered in two weeks, but it's now been four weeks and we still haven't received anything.

Jose: I do apologize for that. You should have an order number on your invoice. Could I please have that number?

Fely: Sure, it's J83L85RS20.

Jose: Thank you for that. OK, let me see what happened. It seems there has been a _____ error. I am sorry for the inconvenience. We will get this fixed _____, and I can assure you that this kind of mistake won't happen again.

VOCABULARY

Find the verb in the vocabulary list with the same meaning and write it on the line.

1. fix _____

2. break _____

3. place responsibility _____

4. deal with _____

5. take _____

PRACTICE

Correct the mistake in each of the following sentences.

1. I'm calling to make a <u>complain</u>.
2. A mistake was <u>maked</u> with an order we recently placed.
3. Could you <u>explained</u> what the problem is?
4. I <u>sorry</u> for the inconvenience.
5. I can <u>sure</u> you that this won't happen again.

12 Closing a Call

Learning Objectives

- To learn vocabulary for ending calls
- To use a range of phrases to close a call
- To learn and practice language signals for ending a call

WARM-UP

1. What do you usually say at the end of a work-related call?
2. What is some basic information you need to provide at the end of a call?
3. What is a polite way to inform someone you want to end a call?

Vocabulary

NOUNS

cooperation
lookout
note / point
patience
response
summary
indicator

VERBS

keep an eye out
leave it
look forward to
put down
(have to) run
run through

ADJECTIVES

beneficial
efficient
grateful
high

ADVERBS

abruptly
alternatively
mutually

Closing a Call — A Process

Confirming the result

- Alright. I'll put that down on my calendar.
- Let's just run through a summary of what we discussed.

Promising action

- OK. I'll send a response...

Closing the call

- I think that's everything.
- Is there anything else?
- Let's leave it at that for the moment.
- I'm sorry to end so abruptly, but I have to run because...

Thanking

- Thanks for calling (back).
- Thank you for your patience.
- I'm very grateful for your cooperation.

Ending on a high note

- I think this worked out in the most efficient way possible.
- I'll be on the lookout for your email.
- Please keep an eye out for my follow-up email.
- Looking forward to talking / working with you again soon!
- I think this has been very mutually beneficial.

Saying goodbye

- See you. Goodbye!
- Talk to you again soon!

Give a Closing Indicator	Anyway,...	Alright...	OK. Well,...	So,...
	Anyway, I'm sorry to end abruptly, but I have to run because...	**Alright**. Is there anything else?	**OK. Well**, let's leave it at that for the moment.	**So**, I think that's everything.

DIALOG

Fill in the blanks. Listen and check. Track 1-12

Alright	run through	cooperation	Alternatively

Tara: Let me quickly just _____ our schedule again. The Thursday morning meeting has been postponed until Monday afternoon at 3 o'clock. Is that right?

Vanessa: That's right. I'll send you an email by this Friday to confirm that time again.

Tara: OK. Thank you. I'll be on the lookout for that. _____, you can just text me, if that's easier.

Vanessa: Alright. I'm sorry about having to change our schedule. Thanks for your _____.

Tara: It's no problem. _____, I have to run to an appointment. I look forward to seeing you Monday.

Vanessa: OK. Thanks again for your patience. See you on Monday.

Tara: Absolutely. Goodbye.

VOCABULARY

Circle the word that does not belong in each group.

1.	close	end	run	finish
2.	slowly	abruptly	suddenly	quickly
3.	signal	indicator	summary	sign
4.	difficult	beneficial	helpful	good
5.	ignore	keep an eye out	be on the lookout	wait for

PRACTICE

Choose the best word to complete each sentence.

1. Let's quickly _____ what we discussed.
   a. run   b. run through   c. leave it   d. keep an eye out for

2. Right. I'll send you a _____ by Friday.
   a. lookout   b. cooperation   c. high   d. response

3. _____, you can just call me if it's more convenient.
   a. Actively   b. Alternatively   c. Abruptly   d. Mutually

4. Sorry, but I have to _____.
   a. run   b. look forward to   c. keep an eye out   d. put down

5. Thank you for your _____.
   a. grateful   b. efficient   c. patience   d. indicator

13 Calls in Different Cultures

Learning Objectives

- To learn vocabulary for cross-cultural calls
- To recognize different cultural approaches to calls
- To learn skills for deciding appropriate levels of formality

WARM-UP

1. How often do you have calls with people from other countries or cultures?
2. What are some cross-cultural considerations you should make?
3. What are some good ways to learn about another culture?

Vocabulary

NOUNS

directness
expectations
friendliness
humor
indifference
professionalism
punctuality
silence

VERBS

clarify
disturb
enable
guarantee
interrupt
notify
respect

ADJECTIVES

personal
safe
simple

ADVERBS

concisely
thoroughly

Cross-Cultural Tips — A Checklist

What are the cultural differences and similarities?

- ☐ Thoroughly learn as much as possible about the country, company, and people you'll be talking to and show respect for their culture.

Is time viewed as a scarce or unlimited resource?

- ☐ Try to clarify and meet cultural expectations in regards to following the scheduled agenda, or accepting unexpected things being added to the agenda.
- ☐ Be patient if there is silence, as it means different things in different cultures: agreement, disagreement, indifference, etc.

How important is formality?

- ☐ Using last names is safer, as they are more formal.
- ☐ In some cultures, being overly friendly at work can be considered unprofessional.
- ☐ Idioms and humor can be culturally specific and difficult to understand. Use clear and simple language.
- ☐ Directness can be seen as rude.

International video conferencing

- ☐ Check the local time of the office you are calling.
- ☐ Not everyone has a high level of English. Speak slowly and concisely to guarantee understanding.
- ☐ Be careful not to interrupt or disturb others while they are speaking.

> **Biz Tip**
>
> *If your business relationship with another person is on a "first name basis," then it's OK to be professional yet more informal.*

More Formal	Mr. / Ms. + last name	I am...	Thank you
More Informal	first name	I'm...	Thanks

30

DIALOG

Fill in the blanks. Listen and check. `Track 1-13`

safer	Mr.	guarantee	respect

Natsuko: I'm a little worried about calling Mr. Sanchez in Mexico. I don't know anything about Mexican culture. Do you have any suggestions?

Louis: Well, I've heard it's good to start with small talk before you get down to business. Many Americans _____ directness, but other cultures may not.

Natsuko: Is it appropriate for me to call him "_____" or should I use "señor"?

Louis: I think Mr. is the _____ title to use.

Natsuko: I'm also worried I might not understand his accent.

Louis: I _____ you won't understand everything. But don't worry. Just ask him to repeat or clarify and then concisely summarize your notes before you hang up. This will enable him to notify you if any details are missing, or if there has been any misunderstanding.

VOCABULARY

Match the words that have the same meaning.

1. friendliness •
2. indifference •
3. enable •
4. thoroughly •
5. silence •

• a. not caring
• b. niceness
• c. completely
• d. complete quiet
• e. allow

PRACTICE

Fill in the blanks with the correct word.

directness	concisely	humor	interrupt	Ms.

1. Many Americans value _____ when communicating.

2. I think it's better to use her last name and the title "_____."

3. Make sure your notes are _____ organized before you end the call.

4. Listen carefully, and be careful not to _____ her while she's speaking.

5. Keep your communication simple and avoid using _____.

Learning Objectives

- To review key vocabulary for work calls
- To review best practices for business calls
- To practice & review prepositions, abbreviations, and other language useful for calls

WARM-UP

1. What do you need to prepare for a call at work?
2. How can you decide the appropriate level of formality for a call?
3. What do you need to do before, during, and after a call?

Vocabulary

NOUNS

action
availability
chat
contact
participant
purpose
result
tool

VERBS

assure
clarify
follow up
greet
host
identify
interrupt
receive
schedule

ADJECTIVES

appropriate
brief

ADVERBS

abruptly

Business Tips for Calls — Dos & Don'ts

		Do	Don't
Before the call		schedule the call and confirm the availability of the participants	use personal contact information
		send important information to help the other person prepare	send irrelevant information
At the start of the call		greet the other party and make some small talk (if culturally appropriate)	forget to identify yourself and your company
		clarify the purpose of the call	skip discussing the agenda
During the call		take down brief notes to refer to after the call is finished	interrupt the other person
		leave and receive contact information	forget to use hosting tools, such as the chat
At the end of the call		confirm the results of the call	fail to confirm actions to be taken
		thank the other party	end the call too abruptly
After the call		review and write notes	forget to review notes
		follow up	delay following up

Language	Prepositions of Place	Formality	Abbreviations
Words	on, in, via	More: I am / Thank you	FYI / IMO / e.g.
Examples	**on** the internet / phone **in** the chat / agenda **via** Skype / email	Less: I'm / Thanks	**FYI**: For your information **IMO**: In my opinion **e.g.**: For example

DIALOG

Fill in the blanks. Listen and check. `Track 1-14`

follow up	host	assure	via

Ted: Are we ready to go for the conference call _____ Skype tomorrow morning with the new customers from Japan?

Winny: Yes, we're ready.

Ted: Did you check the device in the meeting room?

Winny: Yes, I checked it out. I did a test call to make sure it's working well. I also tested out the hosting tools since I will be the _____ of this meeting.

Ted: That sounds good. We need a good result from this call, and this is a new customer, so let's try to keep the discussion a bit more formal and culturally appropriate.

Winny: Right. I _____ you that I'll do my best to create a positive atmosphere for all the participants.

Ted: Great. I think we should also take down brief notes during the call so we can refer to them after.

Winny: Right! Then we can _____ with them after the call if needed.

Ted: Exactly. OK. I think we are ready. Thank you for preparing everything.

VOCABULARY

Find the word in the vocabulary list with the same meaning and write it on the line.

1. short _____

2. suddenly _____

3. welcome _____

4. timetable _____

5. reason _____

PRACTICE

Fill in the blanks with the correct word.

appropriate	tools	clarify	participants	result

1. I checked out the hosting _____ and they work well.

2. We need a good _____ from the conference call.

3. Try to be more formal and keep the discussion to culturally _____ topics.

4. I will try to make all of the _____ on the call feel comfortable.

5. If you don't understand something, be sure to ask a question to _____ it.

Part **A** Background

Understand that there are several important cultural differences that will impact how successfully you are able to communicate on a call. Being aware of the differences and similarities, and knowing how to prepare for them, can have a big impact on how productive your calls are. Don't assume your clients, colleagues, partners, and others from overseas will know anything about your culture. Be proactive and learn about their culture first in order to understand and effectively deal with cultural differences and similarities.

Part **B** Task

Imagine you work for a company that sells goods and services to customers in the US. Management has recently decided to offshore the customer service call center to cut costs. You have been tasked with choosing a suitable country for the call center and planning a training program that will help the new customer service representatives communicate with your customers effectively.

Work with a partner. Choose a country from the list and learn about its culture. Consider which cultural differences could lead to miscommunications, mistakes, and misunderstandings between your customers and customer service representatives.

Choose a country from the list to offshore your call center to.

the Philippines	Spain	Germany	Mexico	Lithuania
India	Canada	Costa Rica	Hungry	Chile
Poland	China	Malaysia	Colombia	Your choice:
Ireland	Romania	Brazil	France	

Work with a partner. Do research about the business communication culture of the country you choose. Preview the questions in **Part C** and write notes.

> **Notes:**
> • *They tend to think of time as an unlimited resource.*

Part C Compare and Contrast

Try to find the answers to the questions below. Compare and contrast the culture of your chosen country with the culture of your customers. Write your findings.

How important is punctuality?	Call center staff: Time is seen as an unlimited resource.	How is directness viewed?	
	Customers: Time is seen as a scarce resource.		
Is silence acceptable?		Are interruptions acceptable?	
What level of formality is best?		Other:	

Part D Write Training Materials

With a clear understanding of the business communication culture in the country that will host your new customer service call center, and with an overview of the cultural similarities and differences between the customer service representatives and your customers, make a rough draft of the training materials.

	Acceptable / Preferable Communication Behavior	Unacceptable / Discouraged Communication Behavior
Punctuality & time:	Work quickly. Apologize if something takes time. Offer to call back if it takes longer than 1 minute.	
Level of formality:		
Directness, interruptions, & silence:		
Other:		

Part E Role-Play Discussion

Work with a new partner. Compare and discuss the training materials you prepared in **Part D**. Assign each person a role as either a customer service representative or a customer. Role-play a customer complaint call following the directions in the training materials above.

Tip Review appropriate language for complaints on p. 26.

English for Business Writing

WARM-UP

1. What types of business documents and materials do you typically write in English?

2. Do you usually do research, writing, and editing for business documents individually, or do you collaborate with colleagues?

3. What strategies can you and your team use to improve your business English writing?

01 Successful Writing

Learning Objectives

- To learn vocabulary for business-related writing
- To recognize the sequence of professional writing
- To learn skills for deciding when writing is preferable to talking

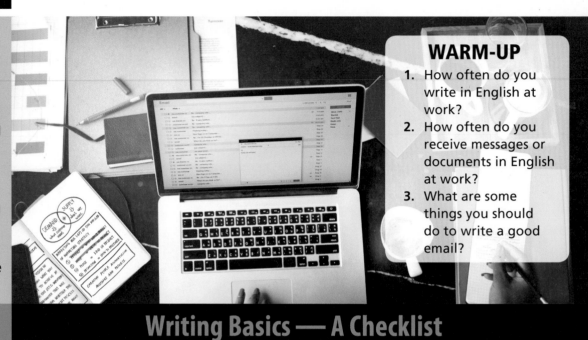

WARM-UP

1. How often do you write in English at work?
2. How often do you receive messages or documents in English at work?
3. What are some things you should do to write a good email?

Vocabulary

NOUNS
content
familiarity
jargon
punctuation
tone

VERBS
adapt
amend
decide
draft
establish
evaluate
link

ADJECTIVES
concise
dynamic
essential
related
relevant
unnecessary

ADVERBS
absolutely
specifically

Writing Basics — A Checklist

Writing process

Plan before you write → Consider the reader → Structure the information → Select the right language → Draft, evaluate, and amend → Send

Plan before you write

- ☐ Establish a clear objective.
- ☐ Decide what essential ideas should be included.
- ☐ Write to get the answer you want.

Consider the reader

- ☐ Include only relevant information.
- ☐ Adapt style and tone to the reader's specific relationship to you, professional position, level of familiarity with the topic, and cultural background.

Structure the information

- ☐ Plan a logical sequence and organize different ideas into paragraphs.
- ☐ Link related ideas together with connecting words and phrases.

Select the right language

- ☐ Be concise and avoid jargon.
- ☐ Be careful not to repeat words more than is absolutely necessary.
- ☐ Pay attention to grammar, spelling, and punctuation.

Draft, evaluate and amend, then send

- ☐ Give yourself time to review content, format, language, and style.
- ☐ Check grammar, punctuation, and spelling again.

Expression	the long and the short of it	to get the picture	to get sidetracked
Meaning	the main idea within a longer / complicated message	to comprehend and understand the main idea within a message	to lose focus of the main idea by concentrating more on a smaller thing

DIALOG

Fill in the blanks. Listen and check. `Track 2-01`

long and short of it	jargon	specifically	relevant

Ji-Young: Did you see the message posted on the company's online bulletin board this morning?

Mario: I saw something there this morning, but I didn't understand it. It was too long, and it didn't look like it was related to my department. What was it about?

Ji-Young: Yes, it was long. It had a lot of _____ in it too. The _____ is that there's a government inspection of our warehouse next week.

Mario: Well, that's not really _____ for us since we work in the office. I wonder why HR decided to post it on the bulletin board instead of just telling the warehouse workers?

Ji-Young: Maybe they thought it was just a bit easier to put it in writing for everyone to see.

Mario: Yeah, that's true. Still, I think they could have just emailed everyone in their department. I don't want to get sidetracked reading stuff that's not _____ about my work.

VOCABULARY

Choose the best word or phrase to match the meaning of the underlined words.

1. Could you <u>change</u> the wording in your email a little bit?

   a. adapt   b. decide   c. establish   d. link

2. I like the <u>style</u> of your message to the design department.

   a. punctuation   b. draft   c. concise   d. tone

3. What is the best way to <u>connect</u> two ideas in my writing?

   a. evaluate   b. decide   c. link   d. establish

4. The contents of your blog post are <u>totally</u> right.

   a. absolutely   b. dynamic   c. related   d. concise

5. I don't have any <u>background knowledge about</u> the contents of the letter.

   a. punctuation   b. familiarity with   c. tone   d. jargon

PRACTICE

Fill in the blanks with the correct word.

punctuation	sidetracked	contents	unnecessary	related

1. Did you see the _____ of the message posted on Slack?

2. I didn't really try to understand it because it doesn't seem _____ to my work.

3. Quotation marks, commas, and other _____ make a big difference in writing.

4. There was too much jargon in the message, and they repeated too many _____ words that basically mean the same thing.

5. I got completely _____ trying to understand the message.

02 Organizing Information

Learning Objectives

- To learn vocabulary for organizing writing
- To understand best practices for the organization of ideas
- To practice using prepositions related to writing at work

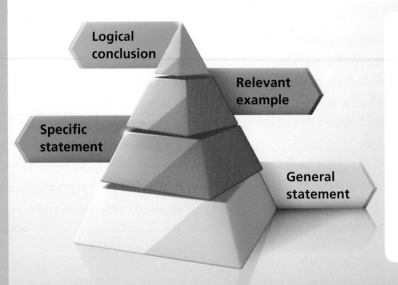

WARM-UP

1. What is the first thing you usually do when you need to write a document or message for work?
2. How should you prepare for work-related writing?
3. What are the best ways to organize your ideas before writing?

Vocabulary

NOUNS

chronology
conclusion
development
effect
introduction
method
outline
process
pyramid
report
sequence
stage
technique

VERBS

brainstorm
prioritize
propose

ADJECTIVES

general
practical
promotional

ADVERBS

steadily

Organizing Your Writing — A Process

Planning

Work in five stages:

1. Write down your objective.
2. Brainstorm possible content.
3. Prioritize and select information.
4. Prepare an outline with main points.
5. Fill in the details and start writing.

Method

There are many different ways to structure information. Here are some common techniques:

1. **Structure:** Like the construction of a pyramid, begin with the most general information and move steadily to more detailed information.
2. **Chronology:** Present in the order that the events took place.
3. **Flow:** Move from problem to solution, cause to effect, etc.
4. **Sequence:** Clearly mark the order of a process of connected things with signposting language (first, second, third).
5. **Segments**: beginning, middle, and end

   I = Introduction
   State the reason for communication and activate any necessary background information.

   II = Development
   Explain further details and other important information.

   III = Conclusion
   Propose a practical solution, next step, required action, etc.

Prepositions	Omit the same preposition that's used multiple times in a parallel structure.	Do not repeat the same preposition over and over.
	I am writing an email **with** sales, marketing, and promotional information.	I am writing an email **with** sales, **with** marketing, and **with** promotional information.

DIALOG

Fill in the blanks. Listen and check. `Track 2-02`

with	pyramid	practical	report

Kelly: I'm trying to write a _____ for the marketing team about some problems with the new promotional contents. I would like to make sure I structured the message clearly enough. Could you have a look at it and let me know what you think?

Pedro: Sure. So what is it about, specifically?

Kelly: They made some promotional materials that show our customers how to sign up for our new online service. The material shows a _____ that has three parts because there are three stages in the process for signing up for the service. See?

Pedro: Uh-huh, that sounds clear enough. So what's the problem?

Kelly: The problem is that the chronology isn't clearly labeled. The process starts at the top of the pyramid for step one, step two is in the middle, and step three is at the bottom of the pyramid. See?

Pedro: Oh, yes, I see the problem now. Some customers must be trying to start at the bottom of the pyramid, with step three, since it's not concisely labeled.

Kelly: Exactly! Customers are having problems signing up because they are getting confused _____ step one, two, and three.

Pedro: Well, your email looks good, but I do think you need to suggest a _____ solution for fixing the problem. So I would add a part to the conclusion suggesting they label each stage in the sign-up process with numbers.

VOCABULARY

Match the words that have the same meaning.

1. activate •
2. propose •
3. method •
4. brainstorm •
5. sequence •

• a. suggest
• b. order
• c. plan
• d. start
• e. way

PRACTICE

Fill in the blanks with the correct word.

chronology	promotional	outline	conclusion	stages

1. The _____ contents they made had some problems.

2. There are three _____ to the sign-up process.

3. The problem is that the _____ isn't clear enough.

4. Finally, in the _____ you should add a suggestion for how to fix the problem.

5. Before writing, you should prepare an _____ with your main points, and then check it after you write.

03 Business Emails

- To learn vocabulary for business emails

- To understand a range of email formats

- To understand how to use various levels of formality in business emails

COMPOSE

Inbox (1)

Important

Sent Mail

WARM-UP

1. What is a polite and professional way to start an email?
2. Do you have a signoff that you typically use to close your emails with?
3. What are some different email formats you have used?

Vocabulary

NOUNS
attachment
bullet points
caution
discretion
emphasis
salutation
signature

VERBS
carbon copy (cc)
forward
present

ADJECTIVES
adequate
confidential
consistent
dear
private
sensitive
standard
updated
varying

ADVERBS
legally

Business Emails — Dos & Don'ts

People write emails in many different styles with varying levels of formality. Remember that email is not a private method of communication. Use caution and discretion when communicating confidential or legally sensitive information. Here are some dos and don'ts to help you.

Do	Don't
• present short sequences of information clearly with bullet points • enter a precise subject in the subject box • give people adequate time to reply • create a filing system for mail / attachments • add key information in the email signature • call if urgent • keep address book updated • use a consistent and standard salutation	• use a personal or a private email address • use unsecure internet connections or devices • send unnecessary files or messages • forward mail or cc without thinking • write too formally / informally • write in capitals for emphasis • use too many abbreviations / symbols • use email to avoid making a call

Biz Tip

For informal communication, nouns regarding communication can be used as verbs. e.g., I'll email you. To remain more formal, use these words as nouns. e.g., I will send you an email.

Formal	Best regards	Dear	I have	Could we please...?
Informal	Cheers	Hi	I've	Can we...?

EMAIL

Fill in the blanks. Listen and check. `Track 2-03`

attachment	confidential	Can	cc

To: Susan.Jefferson@wjcbiz.com
From: t.choi@wjcbiz.com
CC: Stacey.Lee@wjcbiz.com
Subject: Re: Employee Accountability Report

Hi, Susan,

I'm glad to hear the report was well received by the team leaders at the weekly meeting. _____ you send me that document as an _____? I'd like to review the final version of the report. I also want to keep a copy of it in my _____ files, since the information is sensitive. I know the COO wants to have a look, too, so please _____ Stacey when you email me the report.

Cheers,
Tim

`Send`   A 🔗 😊 🖼   ⋮ 🗑

VOCABULARY

Complete each definition with a word from the vocabulary list.

1. When you want to make something stand out, you give it _____.

2. When you say "hello," you're using a _____.

3. If you want to send someone an email you received, then _____ it to them.

4. Doing things in a similar way every time means you are being _____.

5. When something is good enough, it is _____.

PRACTICE

Rewrite the underlined words to change them from informal to formal.

1. <u>Hi,</u> Susan,

   _____

2. <u>I'm</u> glad the report was well received by the team leaders.

   _____

3. <u>Can you</u> send me that document?

   _____

4. <u>I'd</u> like to have a look.

   _____

5. <u>Thanks,</u>

   _____

04 Correspondence Phrases

Learning Objectives

- To learn vocabulary for email correspondence
- To use set phrases to correspond by email
- To learn and practice skills for corresponding via email

WARM-UP

1. How often do you use email for correspondence?
2. What topic is your work correspondence usually about?
3. What are some phrases that you regularly use while corresponding?

Vocabulary

NOUNS

assistance
conversation
correspondence
expression
inconvenience
manufacturing
refund

VERBS

enclose
experience
hesitate
inquire
regret
shall

ADJECTIVES

delighted
elaborate
further
grateful
pleased

ADVERBS

deeply
unfortunately

Reasons for Correspondence — Useful Phrases

Starting expressions

With reference to your email,...	Regarding our meeting last week,...	Regarding our conversation,...

Reason for writing

We are writing to inquire about...	I'm just writing to inform...	Just a short note to confirm...

Giving good / bad news

We are delighted to inform you... You will be pleased to hear that...		We regret to inform you that... I am afraid that... / Unfortunately,...

Making a request

We would appreciate it if you could...	I'd be grateful if you could...	Could you please... (elaborate)?

Offering help

If you wish, we would be happy to...	Would you like me to...? / Shall I...?	I have enclosed... to help you.

Apologizing

We must apologize for (not) ... / We deeply regret...	I do apologize for... (any inconvenience caused).	I'm really sorry for / about...

Closing remarks

Do not hesitate to contact us again if you need further assistance.	If you have any further questions, please contact me.	Let me know if you need any more help.

Positive Future Reference	We look forward to meeting / seeing you next week.	We look forward to hearing from you.	We look forward to future cooperation.

EMAIL

Fill in the blanks. Listen and check. `Track 2-04`

grateful	We look forward to	inconvenience	delighted

Dear Ms. Strait,

We regret the problem you experienced with the Fun Flash 300X. We are _____ for your bringing this problem to our attention. The manufacturing problem has been corrected. We apologize for any _____ this has caused you.

We are _____ to offer you a full refund and a year of free online Fun Flash 300X storage of up to 300 gigabytes.

We hope that you will use this offer and see the true quality of our products and services. Please do not hesitate to contact us if you have any more problems. _____ continuing to serve your needs as a valued customer in the future.

Sincerely,
Kevin Stills
Customer Service Representative
Fun Flash Cameras
7750 Beltway St., Carson, OH 44277, USA
phone: (365)972-3350 fax: (365)972-3351

> **Biz Tip**
> Try to end with a positive and constructive tone, even if the correspondence is about something negative.

VOCABULARY

Circle the word that does not belong in each group.

1. shall	inquire	will	going to
2. further	more	additional	far
3. hesitate	wait	hold	process
4. deeply	lowly	sincerely	very
5. conversation	talk	help	discussion

PRACTICE

Fill in the blanks with the correct word.

experience	manufacturing	inquire	refund	regret

1. We _____ the problem you had.

2. The _____ issue has been fixed.

3. We would like to offer you a full _____.

4. We apologize you had this inconvenient _____.

5. If there are any more issues or questions, please feel free to _____ directly.

Learning Objectives

- To learn vocabulary for creating official documents
- To recognize best practices for contract and MOU writing
- To understand appropriate levels of formality for different document types

WARM-UP

1. How often do you make or receive contracts at work?
2. What is the difference between a contract and an MOU?
3. What information do you need before writing a contract?

Vocabulary

NOUNS

client
custody
guideline
inconsistency
irregularity
obligation
party
preparation
terminology

VERBS

approximate
assume
coordinate
speculate
strengthen
supervise

ADJECTIVES

binding
colloquial

ADVERBS

from scratch
intuitively
widely

Official Document Writing — Dos and Don'ts

		Do	Don't
Preparation		use guidelines and a professional format that works for many contracts	write each new contract from scratch
		collect all necessary information	approximate and speculate about any information
Organization		have a different section for each obligation (work, payment, etc.)	mix obligations across multiple sections
		make references to specific parts of the contract	assume others will intuitively know what something refers to
Terminology		use only formal language	use slang, jargon, or colloquial language—even if it is widely understood by everyone
		coordinate terms such as "client" or "customer"	use many different words for the same thing
Strengthen		have other, experienced parties review and improve contracts and MOUs	use the first draft as the final draft
		check spelling, grammar, numbering, etc.	leave any mistakes, inconsistencies, or irregularities

Format	contract	MOU	report	internal email
Style	legal / formal / binding	formal / non-binding	standard	professional / informal
Example Language	to take custody of	to ensure protection	to supervise	to take care of

CONTRACT

Fill in the blanks. Listen and check. `Track 2-05`

contract	Client	takes custody	parties

Section III. Delivery of Payment

Clause A:

_____ does not pay Supplier any expenses related to taxes, duties, tariffs, or any other costs associated with the shipment, transportation, customs, or other associated fees.

Client agrees to pay Supplier a total Payment of US $60,000 upon delivery of the Shipment with the following conditions met:

Condition III. A-1: Client _____ of full Shipment, and Shipment meets delivery specifications in Appendix B.

Condition III. A-2: Client receives Shipment no later than one month as of the execution of this _____.

All terms of Section III of this contract are legally binding and final upon the mutual agreement and signatures of both _____, the Client and the Supplier.

The provisions of this Contract shall be governed by and construed in accordance with the laws of the United States of America, and the Republic of California, whose courts shall be courts of competent jurisdiction.

Biz Tip

Remember to follow the POTS acronym: Preparation, Organization, Terminology and Strengthen.

VOCABULARY

Match each word with the correct meaning.

1. speculate •   • a. commonly used

2. from scratch •   • b. from the beginning

3. strengthen •   • c. make stronger or better

4. guideline •   • d. guess

5. colloquial •   • e. suggestion

PRACTICE

Put the following writing steps in logical order (a = first, e = last).

1. _____ use only formal language

2. _____ collect all necessary information

3. _____ have a different section for each obligation (work, payment, etc.)

4. _____ have other, experienced parties review and improve contracts and MOUs

5. _____ send the contract to the other party in the agreement

06 Promotional Materials

Learning Objectives

- To learn vocabulary related to sales, marketing, and promotion
- To use a variety of writing styles to promote a product
- To examine various formats for product promotion

WARM-UP

1. Where are some of the places we see promotional materials?
2. What are some different styles of promotion?
3. What information should be included in promotional materials?

Vocabulary

NOUNS

analytics
asset
audience
awareness
channel
demographics
feedback
format
marketing
platform
pop-up
presence
script

VERBS

customize
post
supply
utilize

ADJECTIVES

educational
promotional

ADVERBS

regularly

Promotional Materials — Common Formats

Social media platforms

use multiple social media platforms	use social media platforms to build customer awareness and brand identity
adapt marketing material to the strength of each platform	write and coordinate posts across platforms

Blogs

write and post regularly to your blog	supply educational and informative content while utilizing pop-up ads
build a strong online following and presence	invite guest bloggers to write posts

Video

create a marketing channel and create a variety of video formats	write scripts and post various formats on a regular schedule
use channel analytics and data as an asset that helps you to customize new video content	use demographic data and feedback to learn more about your audience and customers

Use Active Voice to Encourage Customers	You **helped** us...	The feedback you **gave** us is valuable.	We **hope** to see you again.

POST

Fill in the blanks. Listen and check. `Track 2-06`

channel	customers	audience	feedback

Hello, valued _____,

We want to thank all of you for tuning into the live stream that we did last week on our video _____. We enjoyed demonstrating our new product lineup of smart home appliances for you. Many _____ members participated in the live stream and left comments on the video. We got a lot of valuable _____ from you, and we are planning a series of three more videos based on your requests. Don't forget to share last week's video and this week's blog posts with friends and family. We hope to see you all again next week. Thank you!

VOCABULARY

Choose the best word to match the meaning of the underlined words.

1. Very good information and data about our customers is an <u>advantage</u> for us.
    a. audience   b. channel   c. pop-up   d. asset

2. We should <u>often</u> make posts on our social media pages.
    a. educational   b. regularly   c. promotional   d. marketing

3. Information about your clients is only good if you <u>use</u> it to create new promotional materials.
    a. utilize   b. post   c. supply   d. customize

4. We must <u>give</u> enough information and support to our customers.
    a. create   b. utilize   c. feedback   d. supply

5. The more we post online, the greater <u>knowledge</u> people will have about our company.
    a. format   b. demographics   c. awareness   d. channel

PRACTICE

Rewrite each sentence to change it from passive to active voice.

1. Our customers are thanked for their feedback.

    _____

2. The live stream was viewed by most of the people who had signed up.

    _____

3. Many comments were written by our followers.

    _____

4. Valuable feedback was left by you.

    _____

5. Three more videos were planned by our team.

    _____

07 Business Reports

Learning Objectives

- To learn vocabulary for business reports

- To recognize best practices for business report writing

- To use prefixes to help improve report writing

WARM-UP

1. What is a business report?
2. Why do we make business reports?
3. How often do you write business reports?

Vocabulary

NOUNS

appendix (appendices)
budget
bullet points
executive summary
figure
font
heading
indentation
investigation
recommendation
scope
size
table
title

VERBS

justify
update

ADJECTIVES

alphabetical
fixed
relative

ADVERBS

logically

Writing Reports — A Checklist

Informal reports: to update people on projects, budgets, etc.

There is no fixed format. Simply present information clearly and logically.

Research reports: to present findings of research / investigation

☐ Title page:
Include title, name of writer, date, and reference.

☐ Contents list:
Include all headings / sub-headings with page numbers. Indentation and font size is used to show relative importance of headers.

☐ (Executive) summary:
Review key points. People will then decide if they should read the report.

☐ Methods of investigation:
Explain how you researched the report and how you justify your conclusions.

☐ Introduction:
State the report's objective, scope, and limitations.

☐ The body of the report:
Present findings, recommendations, and conclusions, often with separate headings.

☐ Appendices:
Include tables of figures, illustrations, etc.

☐ References:
Number references to sources, then list them at the end of sections.

☐ Index:
List key words in alphabetical order with page number of use.

Prefixes	sub-	dis-	re-	in-
Meaning	under / slightly	apart / to stop	again / back	not / into

REPORT

Fill in the blanks. Listen and check. **Track 2-07**

sub-	investigation	headings	recommendations

Executive Summary

In response to a recent message posted within the department, an _____ of employee attitudes was launched.

The investigation was done through a survey in which employees could give _____ based on a list of questions with fixed responses. Employees were also asked to provide ideas and opinions for improving accountability. Employee responses are listed in the tables in the appendices. This report discusses the findings of the survey along with the obvious limitations of this study.

There are two major parts of this report, as you will see from the _____ and bullet points below.

First are employee attitudes toward their _____ ordinates working below them. Second are employee attitudes toward personal accountability in the company.

VOCABULARY

Find and write a word from the vocabulary list that has the same meaning as the underlined word.

1. What is the <u>name</u> of that report? _____

2. How do you <u>explain</u> the findings in your report? _____

3. Please send the report that has the <u>money plan</u> for the new project. _____

4. Are these <u>numbers</u> accurate? _____

5. The purpose of the report is to <u>inform</u> you about the progress of our research. _____

PRACTICE

Match each sentence with the word or phrase that best completes it.

1. The employee survey had ____ answers.   •   • a. table

2. The responses are in a ____.   •   • b. fixed

3. All of the tables and ideas are in the ____ at the end of the report. •   • c. alphabetical

4. The headings and ____ list all the main findings.   •   • d. bullet points

5. The names of the employees are in ____ order.   •   • e. appendices

08 Job Openings

Vocabulary

NOUNS

applicant
benefit
circumstance
distinction
duty
environment
growth
incentive
leave
preference
requirement

VERBS

earn
exaggerate
cope
hire
scale up

ADJECTIVES

additional
financial
functional

ADVERBS

succinctly

WARM-UP

1. Where do you go to look for job openings?
2. What kind of information do you expect to see for a job opening?
3. Have you ever written an ad for a job opening?

Job Opening Ads — A Checklist

A good job opening advertisement should include the following:

Specific information about the role

☐ Detail where the work must be done and the expectations of applicants.
☐ Detail working hours, responsibilities, etc.

Distinctions between requirements and preferences

☐ List requirements, such as educational requirements, that each applicant must meet.
☐ List other preferences such as level of experience, certifications, language abilities, etc.

Accurate descriptions of functional work

☐ Do not exaggerate or understate explanation of duties; explain them as accurately and succinctly as possible.

A clear list of challenges and benefits

☐ Describe the work environment, hours, and other circumstances employees who work at your company must be ready to cope with.
☐ Explain financial compensation, paid leave, bonuses, and additional incentives employees can earn.

Information about the direction of your company

☐ Describe the size of your company and how long it has been operating.
☐ Explain the reason for hiring new employees (e.g., scaling up for growth).

Instructions about how, when, and where to apply

☐ Request the precise documents, formats, etc., that you wish to receive from applicants.
☐ Inform possible applicants of the start and end of the application period.
☐ Include contact information for accepting applications.

Descriptive Phrases	competitive salary	bonus package	perks (informal)
Meaning	a fair salary	a set of incentives	small benefits employees can enjoy

JOB AD

Fill in the blanks. Listen and check. Track 2-08

scaling	competitive salary	hired	growth

Position: Project Manager

Employer: WJC Construction & Engineering

About the Employer & Employment Opportunity:

WJC C&E is a South Korea-based global construction and engineering company. Founded in 1985, we have built a wide range of development specialties. With successful infrastructure projects in over 50 countries, we are _____ up to meet the demand for sustainable energy projects around the world. If you are interested in an exciting career with a stable company that is experiencing rapid _____, and provides a _____ and other perks, then please follow the link below to our website, which has all of the specifics about the position and how to apply. You can also read testimonials from employees who have already been _____. We hope to hear from qualified applicants soon.

VOCABULARY

Circle the word that does not belong in each group.

1. benefit   aid   help   present
2. holiday   vacation   go   leave
3. functional   financial   economic   monetary
4. natural   environment   surroundings   situation
5. preference   wish   desire   requirement

PRACTICE

Choose the best word to complete each sentence.

1. We are looking to _____ a new project manager.
   a. cope   b. exaggerate   c. hire   d. scale

2. All _____ must have a college degree and a project management certificate.
   a. applicants   b. duties   c. preferences   d. leaves

3. You can read a testimonial from employees about the _____ of working at our company.
   a. preferences   b. benefits   c. growth   d. requirements

4. The work _____ at this company is very good, with lots of helpful employees.
   a. growth   b. leave   c. circumstances   d. environment

5. You can read more about the specific _____ expected of each applicant by following the link below.
   a. applicants   b. growth   c. duties   d. circumstances

09 Cover Letters & Résumés

Learning Objectives

- To learn vocabulary for résumé writing
- To learn skills for cover letter and résumé writing
- To recognize language that is unique to résumé writing

WARM-UP

1. How often do you update your résumé?
2. What is the difference between a cover letter and a résumé?
3. Have you ever seen a résumé from another country?

Vocabulary

NOUNS

accomplishment
alma mater
capability
certification
competency
employer
reference
spacing
template

VERBS

attract
demonstrate
distinguish
employ
tailor

ADJECTIVES

centered
chronological
flawless
irrelevant
well-structured

ADVERBS

grammatically

Cover Letters & Résumés — A Checklist

A good cover letter

☐ short, simple, and clear
☐ demonstrates knowledge of the company
☐ attracts the reader with your accomplishments and capabilities
☐ asks for an interview
☐ has flawless spelling, punctuation, grammar, and style

A good résumé

☐ well-structured, simple, and clear
☐ clean, easy to read, and professional-looking
☐ tailored to the place you want to be employed
☐ demonstrates results and competency
☐ free of irrelevant details
☐ without any spelling or punctuation errors
☐ grammatically perfect

Details to include on your résumé

☐ professional contact details
☐ employment history
☐ alma mater (educational history)
☐ professional certifications
☐ professional references
☐ awards and accomplishments

Résumé formatting

☐ information is in chronological order
☐ information is centered
☐ consistent spacing
☐ follows a basic template

> **Biz Tip**
>
> The format of and expected information for a job application or résumé is different depending on the country.

Résumé-Related Terminology	CV = curriculum vitae / longer-form résumé	alma mater = the school that a person attended / education

DIALOG

Fill in the blanks. Listen and check. `Track 2-09`

references	alma mater	irrelevant	template

Janet: I think there are some things you can change to make your résumé better.

Curtis: Alright. So what do you suggest I change first?

Janet: Well, first of all, I think there's too much information here. There are some details the employer may feel are _____.

Curtis: Oh, really? Like what?

Janet: Like your high school education history. For your _____, most companies just want to know about college level and above. Also, you don't need to talk about your hobbies. They can use your _____ to learn more about you as a person and your professional life.

Curtis: I see. Thank you. I guess there are some changes I should make then.

Janet: Yes. And one other thing is using a _____. If you fill out a LinkedIn profile online, you can use that as sort of a basic template for your offline résumé as well.

Curtis: That is a great idea. That will really help to highlight my accomplishments and competencies.

VOCABULARY

Match the words that have the same meaning.

1. employ •
2. flawless •
3. centered •
4. accomplishment •
5. attract •

• a. success
• b. hire
• c. engage
• d. perfect
• e. in the middle

PRACTICE

Fill in the blanks with the correct word or phrase.

competencies	employer	distinguish	accomplishments	alma mater

1. The _____ might not care that your hobbies are golf and hiking.

2. For your _____, they really only want to know about your education after high school.

3. Using a résumé template will help to show my past _____ at other companies.

4. I can show what _____ I have by including the certifications I have earned.

5. A cover letter can help _____ you from the other people applying for a job.

Learning Objectives

- To learn technical vocabulary

- To use a range of vocabulary to give technical instructions

- To practice structures useful for giving instructions

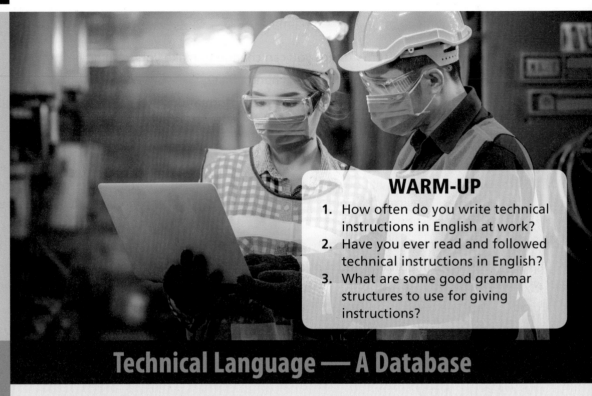

WARM-UP

1. How often do you write technical instructions in English at work?
2. Have you ever read and followed technical instructions in English?
3. What are some good grammar structures to use for giving instructions?

Vocabulary

NOUNS

code
engineer
facility
security
structure
task

VERBS

accommodate
adjust
alter
be composed of
be comprised of
consist of
contain
operate
perform
permit
revise
take care of

ADVERBS

automatically
sufficiently

Technical Language — A Database

Use the following database of keywords to help you create and follow technical instructions, systems, etc.

Concept	Verbs
Structure	Our system <u>is made up of</u> four parts. - is composed of, is comprised of, consists of
Facility	The system <u>lets you</u> offer customizable billing. - allows you to, enables you to, permits you to
Capability	The program will <u>deal with</u> problems sufficiently. - handle, manage, take care of
Tasking	Their software can <u>carry out</u> security tests. - do, execute, perform
Contents	This site can <u>house</u> three electrical units. - accommodate, contain, hold
Change	These codes must be <u>changed</u> by an engineer. - adjusted, altered, revised
Process	The bolt is <u>linked</u> to hydraulic hoses. - connected, hooked up, joined *use passive speech with past participle verb forms to describe an impersonal process

Biz Tip

Imperatives are commonly used to address a wide audience, not a specific person. When talking to a specific persons, use "please" and other such language to make the instructions more polite sounding.

Structure	imperative	must / should	to / in order to
Instructions / Procedure	**Remove** the housing and **install** the fuse.	Surfaces **must** be clean and dry.	**In order to** operate, press start.

INSTRUCTIONS

Fill in the blanks. Listen and check. `Track 2-10`

code	operating	perform	should

Sales Track 6G Installation

Before installing and _____ the software, you _____ make sure your computer contains adequate memory space. Check the technical specifications listed on the next page to be sure Sales Track 6G will run on your computer.

To _____ the installation, simply visit our website and enter the security _____ contained on the inside of the box. If installation does not start automatically, click the download icon, enter the code from inside the box, and then double-click the EXE file displayed. When the download is complete, click the "Run" button on the screen.

VOCABULARY

Match the words that have the same meaning.

1. alter •   • a. job

2. task •   • b. make

3. permit •   • c. allow

4. contain •   • d. change

5. compose •   • e. have

PRACTICE

Choose the best word to complete each sentence.

1. Before installing and using the software, you _____ make sure your device has enough memory available.
   a. would   b. should not   c. must   d. could

2. _____ begin the installation, start by visiting our website.
   a. In order to   b. You must   c. Take care of   d. Accommodate

3. If it doesn't start _____, then click the download icon.
   a. sufficiently   b. security   c. cleanly   d. automatically

4. When the process is finished, _____ the "Run" button.
   a. alter   b. click   c. adjust   d. permit

5. Please contact an _____ for assistance if you experience any problems.
   a. engineer   b. structure   c. facility   d. task

→ *Activity File* page 111

11 Connecting Words

Learning Objectives

- To learn vocabulary for more effective writing

- To use a range of connecting words for more concise and effective writing

- To recognize rules for when it is appropriate to connect ideas

WARM-UP

1. What are some words used to connect ideas in a single sentence?
2. What are some words used to connect ideas between sentences?
3. What kind of punctuation is used when connecting ideas?

Vocabulary

NOUNS

alternative
condition
consequence
flag

VERBS

bring about
contrast
exemplify
generalize
highlight
mention
refer

ADJECTIVES

aforementioned
former
latter
partial

ADVERBS

consequently
effectively
efficiently
respectively
similarly

Connecting Words — Useful Language

Writing effectively and efficiently means knowing how to connect ideas.

Connector functions

sequencing	first, second, third, after that, finally, respectively
adding	in addition, moreover, furthermore
alternatives	alternatively, instead of
consequence	therefore, consequently, as a result
comparing	similarly, in line with
contrasting	however, yet, whereas, although, despite
conditions	if, on condition that, providing, unless
reference	with respect to, regarding, in relation to
reasons	because, since, as, in response to
cause verbs	to lead to, to result in, to bring about, to cause
effect verbs	to result from, to be due to, to be caused by
highlighting	in particular, especially, mainly, chiefly
exemplifying	for example / instance, such as, as follows
generalizing	usually, normally, in general

> **Biz Tip**
>
> FANBOYS = Coordinating conjunctions for, and, nor, but, or, yet, and so.

Text flags

referring forward	below, as you will see, in the following / latter
referring back	above, as mentioned earlier, in the former / aforementioned

Sentence Structure	Use a comma before FANBOYs when combining two independent clauses.
Example	Jessica achieved a record number of sales last year. She won the Employee of the Year Award. → Jessica achieved a record number of sales last year, so she won the Employee of the Year Award.

EMAIL

Fill in the blanks. Listen and check. `Track 2-11`

efficiently	aforementioned	highlight	bring about

Hello, Marshall,

I hope you're doing well. Regarding the employee survey we conducted earlier this month, many employees felt the best way to _____ individual accountability was through special recognition in each department. Employees who work _____ or have outstanding performance can be recognized through "Employee of the Month" awards. Highlighting the performance of employees with good personal accountability may _____ improved performance throughout each department. Consequently, efficiency and performance throughout the whole company will increase.

The _____ recommendation is the most popular idea. However, for your reference, a partial list of the alternative ideas listed by employees in the survey can be found in the latter part of the attachment.

Please let me know if you have any questions.

Sincerely,
Dan

VOCABULARY

Match each word with the correct meaning.

1. exemplify •
2. mention •
3. respectively •
4. similarly •
5. generalize •

• a. in almost the same way
• b. say
• c. be an example of
• d. in the order given
• e. make something basic and simple

PRACTICE

Fill in the blanks with the correct word.

alternative	partial	mentioning	Consequently	latter

1. A list of _____ ideas can be found below.

2. _____, efficiency and performance throughout the whole company will increase.

3. The other employee ideas from the survey can be found in the _____ part of the attachment.

4. That is only a _____ list of the other ideas, not the complete one.

5. The other ideas had little to no support from other employees, so they aren't worth _____.

→ *Activity File* page 112

Learning Objectives

- To learn vocabulary for editing writing
- To identify and correct common spelling and grammar mistakes
- To practice a range of skills related to fixing mistakes

WARM-UP

1. Why is it important to check spelling and grammar?
2. What are some tools you can use to check spelling and grammar?
3. Has anyone ever asked you to check their writing?

Vocabulary

NOUNS

advice
goods
position
procedure
reputation
risk
tense

VERBS

analyze
avoid
edit
mitigate
rely on
remove
solve

ADJECTIVES

countable
nonessential
fundamental
trained

ADVERBS

highly
wrongly

Grammar & Spelling Checks — A Checklist

Avoid mistakes. Edit your own writing with the following checklist.

Checklist	Common Mistakes
☐ **Tense**	The goods ~~have~~ arrived yesterday.
☐ **Subject-verb agreement**	My people ~~is~~ are highly trained.
☐ **Countable or not**	Please analyze ~~these informations~~ this information.
☐ **Modal verbs**	We must ~~to~~ solve this problem soon.
☐ **Adverb or adjective**	Please follow the ~~normally~~ normal procedure.
☐ **Adverb position**	We always have ~~always~~ this problem.
☐ **Preposition**	We must focus ~~at~~ on this at the next meeting.
☐ **Who = people**	She is the person ~~which~~ who mitigates risk.
☐ **Which = things**	Our office, ~~that~~ which is also new, is in Houston.
☐ **That = things**	We have a new office ~~which~~ that is in Houston.

*which is used with nonessential information that if removed, wouldn't change the fundamental meaning of the sentence

*that is used with essential information that, if removed, would change the fundamental meaning of the sentence

Biz Tip

Some countries, such as Canada, use a mix of American and British English spellings and words.

Spelling Differences	-or / -our	-ter / -tre	-ze / -se
American English	labor	center	analyze
British English	labour	centre	analyse

DIALOG

Fill in the blanks. Listen and check. `Track 2-12`

nonessential	reputation	advice	rely on

Travis: Can you check the spelling and punctuation for me one more time? I had a
_____ as a terrible speller in school, so I always worry about it now.

Asef: I usually _____ my computer to check all that for me.

Travis: That works well in general, but I've noticed a few times the computer has suggested I've wrongly written a sentence that is actually correct.

Asef: I've noticed that too. Usually, the problem is related to the use of _____ commas.

Travis: I trust your _____ more than a computer. Do you see anything to edit in my résumé?

VOCABULARY

Find the verb in the vocabulary list with the same meaning and write it on the line.

1. study   _____

2. weaken   _____

3. take away   _____

4. depend on   _____

5. keep away from _____

PRACTICE

Correct the mistake in each of the following sentences.

1. I entered all the data <u>correct</u>, but there still seems to be an error.

2. She <u>is</u> researching customer satisfaction for the last two months, but she needs more time.

3. The people involved in the negotiation <u>is</u> all from Australia.

4. Your fax <u>was arrive</u> over the weekend when the office was closed.

5. The report must <u>to be</u> finished before next Tuesday.

13 Punctuation

WARM-UP

1. When do you need to use accurate punctuation in your writing?
2. When is it OK to ignore punctuation rules in work-related writing?
3. What are some rules about using punctuation such as commas, dashes, etc.?

Vocabulary

NOUNS

clause
decision
disbelief
explanation
irony
possession
ownership
sarcasm

VERBS

contract
enclose
express
introduce
offset
punctuate
separate

ADJECTIVES

correlated
exact
introductory
reported

ADVERBS

closely

Punctuation — A Checklist

Avoid punctuation mistakes. Follow the rules in the checklist.

Checklist	Rules
☐ **Comma ,**	used after introductory words, to separate items in a list, and with a coordinating conjunction to connect two independent clauses
☐ **Colon :**	used to introduce a list of items
☐ **Semicolon ;**	used to connect two sentences or independent clauses which are closely correlated
☐ **Apostrophe '**	used to show possession, ownership, or relationship used to contract two words
☐ **Dash / Hyphen -**	used to offset nonessential information used to join adjectives, names, or numbers
☐ **Quotations " "**	used to designate exact, reported speech or specific names used to express disbelief, irony, or sarcasm
☐ **Parenthesis ( )**	used to enclose extra information such as an example, reference, or brief explanation

*The Oxford comma is a comma that is often used after the second to last item in a list of three or more things, before the word "and" or "or." Whether or not to use the Oxford comma is a stylistic decision.

Biz Tip

Be aware that punctuation can be called, used, and mean different things in different countries.

Punctuation	@	_	[ ]	/
Name	at symbol	underscore	brackets	forward slash

DIALOG

Fill in the blanks. Listen and check. `Track 2-13`

at symbol	punctuated	introductory	clause

Ji-Young: Could you take a look at this email and tell me if I have _____ it correctly?

Bella: Sure. Which parts do you want me to look at?

Ji-Young: I'm not sure if this sentence needs commas or not.

Bella: I'm not an expert on this, but I think in this case you have an _____ phrase in the sentence. So put a comma here after the phrase. Also, I think you need a comma in the middle of this sentence because it connects a dependent and an independent _____.

Ji-Young: OK, and what about this other sentence? Should I use a colon or semicolon?

Bella: Since you're introducing a list, you need to use a colon.

Ji-Young: OK, and last question. What do you call this symbol in English?

Bella: Oh, easy! That's called an "_____."

VOCABULARY

Circle the word that does not belong in each group.

1.	express	say	tell	ask
2.	exact	precise	careful	accurate
3.	closely	quickly	similarly	nearly
4.	contract	promise	shrink	decrease
5.	correlated	connected	joined	reported

PRACTICE

Match each question with the correct response.

1. Is this punctuated correctly? •

2. Does this sentence need a comma? •

3. Should I put a comma after an introductory phrase? •

4. Should I use a colon or a semicolon here? •

5. What is this thing called? •

• a. Yes, because it connects a dependent and an independent clause.

• b. Since you're introducing a list, you should use a colon.

• c. That's an "at symbol."

• d. Which part are you talking about?

• e. Yes, you should.

→ *Activity File* page 113

Learning Objectives

- To review key vocabulary for business writing
- To review best practices for work-related writing
- To practice & review structures for business writing

WARM-UP

1. What do you need to prepare for writing at work?
2. How can you decide the appropriate level of formality for writing?
3. What do you need to do before, during, and after drafting a document?

Vocabulary

NOUNS

correspondence
guideline
jargon
party
preparation
terminology

VERBS

approximate
assume
coordinate
draft
speculate
strengthen
supervise

ADJECTIVES

appropriate
colloquial
concise
necessary

ADVERBS

from scratch
intuitively
logically

Business Tips for Writing — Dos & Don'ts

		Do	Don't
Preparation		collect all the necessary information, logically plan a sequence, and organize your ideas	speculate, approximate, or make assumptions about any information
		use guidelines and a professional format that works for many types of emails, contracts, and other formal writing	draft a new job advertisement, email, contract, etc., from scratch each time you need one
Organization		have different sections for each idea	mix ideas across multiple sections
		use correspondence phrases to signal different parts and intentions	assume the other party will intuitively know what something refers to
Terminology		use only appropriate language for the type of writing	use slang, jargon, or colloquial language
		use terms and titles consistently throughout the document	use too many abbreviations or symbols
Strengthen		review and improve your writing	use the first draft as the final draft
		check spelling, grammar, numbering, punctuation, etc.	leave any mistakes, inconsistencies, or irregularities

Format	contracts	MOUs	report / résumé / external emails / job ads	technical instructions / promotional materials	internal emails
Style	legal / formal / binding	formal / non-binding	formal / standard	standard	professional / informal
Level	most formal / serious	←——————————————————→			least formal / serious

DIALOG

Fill in the blanks. Listen and check. ◀ Track 2-14

logically	drafted	strengthen	coordinated

Suki: This is the last time I'll ask you to edit my work, I promise.

Albert: I don't mind. How many times have you _____ this document?

Suki: This is the third time, so hopefully it's getting better.

Albert: Right. Well, the first draft wasn't written badly. But looking this over now, I think this draft of the document communicates your ideas more _____. And the way the ideas are linked is more effective and really communicates what you're trying to say.

Suki: I tried to _____ it by following your recommendations from last time. I reviewed the punctuation and _____ the terms.

Albert: Yes, I think this is much clearer and more concise than before. I think this is ready to send to the client.

Suki: Thank you for your help.

Albert: No problem.

> **Biz Tip**
>
> Use the appropriate tone and level of formality for the type of writing you are doing, i.e., decide if the documents should have a formal, standard, or informal tone.

VOCABULARY

Match each word with the correct meaning.

1. party •   • a. commonly used

2. from scratch •   • b. person, group, or organization

3. colloquial •   • c. watch

4. approximate •   • d. estimate

5. supervise •   • e. from the beginning

PRACTICE

Fill in the blanks with the correct word.

preparation	terminology	jargon	appropriate	assume

1. Could you please check the _____ I used in my writing?

2. All of the information is gathered, and the _____ is finished.

3. Do not _____ that people will know what you're talking about.

4. Try to avoid using any _____ in your work-related writing.

5. I think this is _____ to send to the customer now.

CASE STUDY

CHAPTER 02: English for Business Writing
Progress Reports: Valuable or Counterproductive?

Part A Background

Most professionals working today must give progress reports of some kind. The frequency and format of these reports can vary as well as who reads them and why. Regardless of these variations, progress reports are a part of doing business for most people. Another thing that varies about progress reports is how professionals view them. Some professionals see them as valuable, while others see them as unnecessary. Thinking about how to maximize the effectiveness and efficiency of routine tasks like progress reports is what many managers are looking for.

Part B Task

Imagine you work for a company that has an anonymous, online, internal message board. Management asks and encourages employees to share their honest opinions about anything related to their work. Recently, a debate has emerged on the message board about the value of progress reports. Your boss has asked you to review some of the opinions shared on the message board, summarize them, and then share your personal opinions about progress reports: should they be kept as is, improved, or eliminated?

Read the opinions of two employees.

Posted on 8/3	Progress Reports are a Waste of Time!

I think the way we do progress reports is outdated. Every employee spends too much time drafting long reports for their boss. We send them by email but never get any feedback about them. A lot of the information we provide in the reports is the same thing we tell our boss in the morning meetings. In the morning meetings, we can also hear each other's problems and help one another. But the progress reports are sent by email, so there's no chance to do that. We should change our system to make it more open and take less time, or get rid of the progress reports sent by email. We could use the time we spend on reports getting work done!

Posted on 8/5	Progress Reports are Helpful & Valuable

I think we should keep the way we do progress reports the same. It only takes about thirty minutes to draft the written report. Although most of the information is the same as what we talk about in the morning meetings, sometimes new things happen and things change throughout the day. Also, sometimes we need to wait for or get information and report it at the end of the day. While it's true we can help each other with work problems in more open communication, sometimes I prefer to talk to my boss privately about certain issues. I think the information also helps our bosses understand what we are doing and can help them evaluate us and our work.

Part C Preparation

Work with a partner. Discuss the two opinions that were posted to the message board. Summarize the opinions in the graphic organizer below: What are the pros and cons (good things and bad things) mentioned by each party? Are there any areas of agreement? What does each party want?

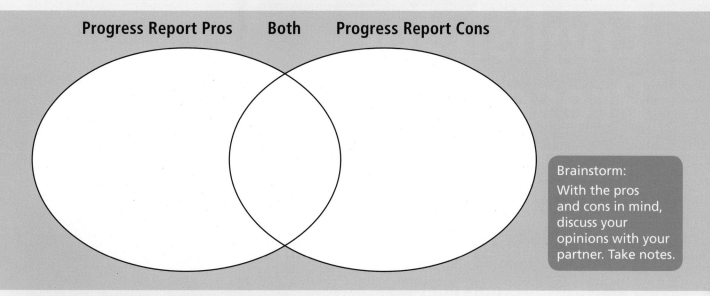

Progress Report Pros   **Both**   **Progress Report Cons**

Brainstorm:
With the pros and cons in mind, discuss your opinions with your partner. Take notes.

Part D Write an Email to Your Boss

With a clear understanding of the views and opinions of your colleagues regarding progress reports, write a rough draft with your opinion. Consider the following questions: Which side do you agree with more? Are there any points you disagree with? Should the progress reports be kept as is, improved, or eliminated? Why do you have that opinion? How do you think your opinion will make / keep the workplace better / good? Also, include other thoughts you may have. Write an email to explain the pros and cons, and offer a possible solution to your boss.

Part E Edit a Partner's Work

Work with a partner. Compare and discuss your emails. Then exchange books and edit each other's writing. Try to find grammar, spelling, and punctuation mistakes. Also, suggest how certain sentences could be changed to improve the writing.

Tip

Review Lessons 11-13; see Lesson 12 for an editing checklist.

English for Presentations

WARM-UP

1. What topics are most commonly discussed during presentations at your workplace?
2. What are the main challenges you face when presenting?
3. What strategies can you and your team use to present more effectively?

01 What Makes a Good Presentation?

Learning Objectives

- To learn vocabulary related to presentations
- To recognize the structure of a presentation
- To learn skills and phrases to help give a good presentation

1. How often do you make presentations in English for work?
2. How often do you listen to presentations in English at work?
3. What are some things that make a presentation effective?

Vocabulary

NOUNS

attitude
complexity
handout
impact
involvement
mannerisms
rhythm

VERBS

conclude
conduct
cover
engage
promote
summarize

ADJECTIVES

allotted
confident
distracting
maximum
nervous
overall

ADVERBS

strategically

Presentation Basics — A Checklist

Presentation process

Greet → Introduce yourself → Introduce topic → Explain presentation structure → Present main body → Conclude → Summarize → Take questions

Remember your audience

☐ Create interest and promote involvement.

Organize the information

☐ Design an overall structure with clear objectives in the introduction.
☐ Make a strong introduction and ending with maximum impact.
☐ Conduct the entire presentation within the allotted time.

Use visuals effectively

☐ Strategically select and place charts, images, etc.
☐ Use visuals to reduce the number of words on a slide.
☐ Provide handouts if appropriate.

Communicate with body language

☐ Be confident and use eye contact to engage your audience.
☐ Focus meaning by using movement and hand gestures.
☐ Avoid nervous and distracting mannerisms.

Deliver your message

☐ Use your voice effectively: volume, rhythm, and pauses.
☐ Adjust complexity / formality of language for the audience.

> **Biz Tip**
>
> *Do not point at people or make obscure hand gestures as they can mean different things in different cultures.*

Common Phrases	body language	eye contact	facial expressions	hand gestures	visuals / visual aids
Examples	upright posture, loose, confident attitude, comfortable	look at various audience members to engage, look at slides to direct audience's attention	raising one eyebrow (skepticism), raising both eyebrows (surprise), smiling, etc.	pointing, waving, counting / listing, balancing, etc.	useful charts, graphs, images, pictures, quotes, etc.

DIALOG

Fill in the blanks. Listen and check. `Track 3-01`

visual aids	complexity	allotted	distracting

Connor: Have you had a chance to look over the handout for my presentation?

Silvia: Yes, and I have some suggestions about the content.

Connor: Really? Do you think I need to adjust the content of the presentation?

Silvia: A little. For instance, I don't think the example you gave in the introduction is really relevant. And the _____ of the last two sections of the presentation may be too much to explain in the _____ time for this presentation.

Connor: I guess I have a lot more work to do on the examples and some of the _____ in the presentation.

Silvia: Maybe after you work on it more, you can practice in front of me.

Connor: Great! You can tell me if I use good body language or have _____ mannerisms.

VOCABULARY

Complete each sentence with a word from the vocabulary list.

1. The _____ of your voice should change depending on the point you're trying to make.

2. You can _____ audience involvement by giving small gifts if they participate.

3. Visuals should be carefully and _____ placed in a presentation.

4. There are a few different methods you can use to ensure you get _____ focus from the audience.

5. If you prepare well for a presentation, you will be confident, not _____.

PRACTICE

Match each sentence with the word that best completes it.

1. Could you take a look at this ____ I made for my presentation? •   • a. conclude

2. Do you think I can ____ the whole presentation with enough time for questions? •   • b. handout

3. ____, I think the presentation is good. •   • c. Overall

4. I'm a little ____ about doing the presentation! •   • d. mannerisms

5. Make sure you practice so you can get rid of any distracting ____. •   • e. nervous

⟶ *Activity File* page 114

Learning Objectives

- To learn vocabulary related to different presentation types

- To understand language that can be used with different kinds of presentations

- To learn phrases to express the purpose of a presentation

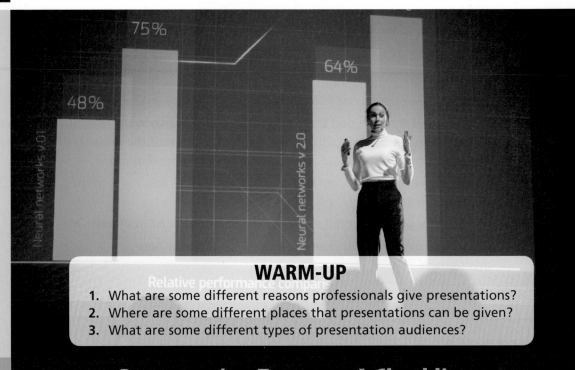

WARM-UP

1. What are some different reasons professionals give presentations?
2. Where are some different places that presentations can be given?
3. What are some different types of presentation audiences?

Vocabulary

NOUNS

discourse
feature
instructions
opinion
product
rhetoric
service
utility
value

VERBS

argue
defend
elevate
persuade
purchase
train

ADJECTIVES

commercial
descriptive
factual
particular
preferable

Presentation Types — A Checklist

Understanding what type of presentation you are doing is an important first step because it can help a lot when deciding what language is best to use. Consider the main purpose of your presentation. What do you want to do?

Inform the audience

- ☐ Give people important factual information.
- ☐ Elevate understanding about a particular topic using discourse.
- ☐ The audience should understand the topic much better.

Persuade the audience

- ☐ Argue that something is preferable to something else.
- ☐ Give your opinion and support it using rhetoric and examples.
- ☐ The audience should understand and defend your standpoint after listening to you.

Sell something to the audience

- ☐ Promote a commercial product or service.
- ☐ Highlight key features, utility, and value using descriptive language.
- ☐ The audience should want to purchase your product.

Train the audience

- ☐ Teach the audience about how to do something.
- ☐ Clearly organize each step and use instructions.
- ☐ The audience should learn how to perform whatever it is you teach.

> **Biz Tip**
>
> After giving the purpose, also say what you're not going to do. e.g., "I'm not here to sell you anything."

Give the Purpose of Your Presentation	My goal today is to inform you about...	Today, I will argue why ... is better than...	After this talk, you will want to buy...	After today's presentation, you will know how to...

DIALOG

Fill in the blanks. Listen and check. `Track 3-02`

My goal is to	purchase	persuade	training

Juan: Are you OK? What are you working on over there?

Samantha: Oh, hey. Yeah, I'm alright. Just a little worried. I'm making this presentation, but I don't know if it's any good or not.

Juan: You want me to have a look at it for you?

Samantha: Sure, if you don't mind. That would be great.

Juan: OK. So what's this presentation for anyway?

Samantha: I want management to _____ a better program to enter our sales data into. The one we have now is really old and has a lot of problems.

Juan: Alright, so you're trying to _____ people then. In that case, I think you should get rid of this part here. You don't need to teach people how the program you're using now works.

Samantha: I thought that by _____ them about how it works, they could see why it's not good and then agree to buy a new program for us. But I guess you're right. I'm not trying to teach them. _____ argue why we need a new program.

Juan: I think a better way is to find an actual product you like, explain its features, and then argue why, in your opinion, it has more utility and value for the company.

VOCABULARY

Circle the word that does not belong in each group.

1. commercial	advertisement	industrial	corporate
2. preferable	better	good	product
3. elevate	raise	see	heighten
4. defend	discuss	protect	guard
5. particular	unclear	exact	specific

PRACTICE

Choose the best word to complete each sentence.

1. I'm trying to _____ why we need a new program.

   a. argue   b. defend   c. elevate   d. train

2. You should explain the _____ of the new product you want to use.

   a. instructions   b. discourse   c. products   d. features

3. You should tell management why, in your _____, the other program is better.

   a. rhetoric   b. opinion   c. utility   d. service

4. Managers want to know what kind of _____ it will have for the workers.

   a. rhetoric   b. discourse   c. utility   d. opinion

5. You have to tell them what kind of _____ a new sales program would have for the company.

   a. product   b. opinions   c. value   d. rhetoric

03 Equipment & Environment

Learning Objectives

- To learn vocabulary related to presentation materials

- To recognize the use of various presentation equipment

- To understand situational language related to presentations

Vocabulary

NOUNS
adapter
audio
center
curtain
lighting
outlet
password
podium
pointer
stage
temperature

VERBS
brighten
dim
draw
lower
raise

ADJECTIVES
compatible
enough
perfect

ADVERBS
easily

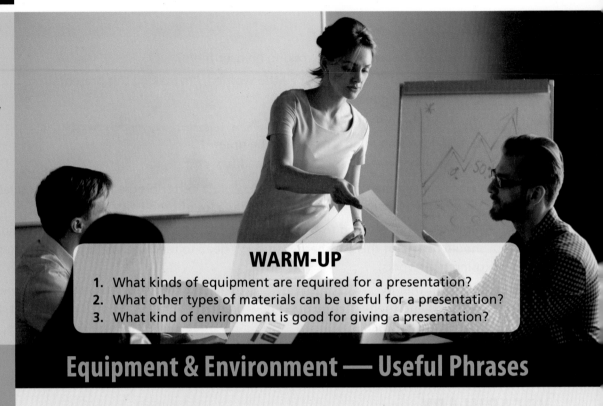

WARM-UP

1. What kinds of equipment are required for a presentation?
2. What other types of materials can be useful for a presentation?
3. What kind of environment is good for giving a presentation?

Equipment & Environment — Useful Phrases

Equipment and materials

- Do you have an adapter for this kind of power cord?
- I think there may be a problem with the audio.
- I'd like to check the display at some point before the presentation.
- Is this compatible with my computer?
- I don't have enough battery to last for the whole presentation.
- She needs a pointer to use during her presentation.
- I have some information prepared for everyone in the audience.
- Do you plan to use markers and a whiteboard during your presentation?
- Here is the microphone you'll be using.
- We've prepared a few bottles of water for you, just in case.

Environment

- Could you point me toward the power outlet?
- Would it be possible to lower / raise the temperature a bit?
- I'd like to move the podium away from the center of the stage.
- Is it alright if we dim / brighten the lighting a bit so people can see easily?
- Let me just draw the curtain so you can see better.
- Can you hear clearly, or should I raise the volume?
- Could you let me know the password for the internet connection?
- The exit is over there, and there's a restroom around the corner.

> **Biz Tip**
> Communicate desired changes and questions about the equipment and environment as polite requests.

Use Polite Requests	Could you...?	Would it be possible to...?	Is it alright if...?

DIALOG

Fill in the blanks. Listen and check. ◀ Track 3-03

podium	temperature	Could you	Perfect

Nick: So here is where you'll be standing during the presentation. Does this look alright to you?

Connie: Actually, would it be alright if we move the _____ a little bit more toward the left side of the stage? I think if it's in the center of the stage, some people might have a difficult time seeing the display.

Nick: Oh, sure. We can certainly do that. We also have the microphone, a bottle of water, and a pointer at the podium as well.

Connie: _____. _____ point me toward an outlet where I can plug in my power cord? The battery on my laptop is terrible.

Nick: Certainly. There's one right over here. And, by the way, this is also where the exit is, and there's a restroom down the hall to the right.

Connie: OK, thanks. And, sorry, just one last thing. Is it possible to lower the _____ a bit during the presentation?

Nick: Absolutely. We will have lunch, and then you can come back here with enough time to test the audio and other things. Does that sound good?

Connie: Yes.

VOCABULARY

Choose the best word to match the meaning of the underlined words.

1. Let's move the display to the <u>middle</u> of the stage.
   a. compatible   b. center   c. enough   d. outlet

2. We should check the <u>brightness</u> before the presentation starts.
   a. temperature   b. stage   c. curtain   d. lighting

3. Can you hear the <u>sound</u> clearly?
   a. audio   b. adapter   c. display   d. pointer

4. Would it be possible to <u>lower</u> the lights a bit?
   a. raise   b. brighten   c. draw   d. dim

5. There will be <u>plenty of</u> time for you to check the audio, display, and other equipment.
   a. clearly   b. compatible   c. enough   d. center

PRACTICE

Match each statement or question with the correct response.

1. Does the stage look alright to you?   •   • a. Thank you.

2. Could you point me toward the outlet?   •   • b. Actually, can we move the podium to the left a bit?

3. We have the microphone, a bottle of water, •   • c. Not really. Could you raise the volume a little?
   and a pointer at the podium as well.

4. Sorry, but is it possible to lower the   •   • d. Yes, we can do that for you.
   temperature a little bit?

5. So can you hear me clearly?   •   • e. Certainly. It's right over here.

Learning Objectives

- To learn vocabulary for beginning a presentation
- To use a range of phrases to open a presentation
- To practice skills for engaging an audience

Vocabulary

NOUNS

aim
attention
comments
market
section
talk
topic

VERBS

begin
comprehend
convince
divide
examine
get started
obtain
outline
split
take a look at

ADJECTIVES

pertinent

ADVERBS

particularly
roughly

WARM-UP

1. What are some different ways to start a presentation?
2. Why is the beginning of a presentation very important?
3. What are the best ways to get the audience's attention?

Starting Your Presentation — A Process

Follow the WISE OWL process to start your presentations.

Welcome the audience

- Good morning / afternoon / evening, ladies and gentlemen.
- Welcome to all of you, and thank you for your attention.

Introduce yourself

- Let me just introduce myself. My name is...
- As some of you know, I'm in charge of... / I'm the CTO at...

Say what the topic is

- Today, we'll be taking a look at / talking about...
- The aim of the topic for today's presentation / discussion is...

Explain why your topic is important

- Today's presentation is particularly pertinent for those who...
- By the end of my talk, you will comprehend... / be convinced...

Outline the structure

- I've divided / split today's presentation / talk into three sections.
- Each part should take roughly thirty minutes.

When each part will come

- First, we'll look at... / Second, we'll discuss... / Third, we'll examine…
- There will also be time for comments / Q&A at the end.

Link to the start

- OK, so let's get started.
- Alright, let's begin by...

> **Biz Tip**
>
> *After the WISE OWL introduction, use one of these hooks to capture the audience's attention.*

Hook	Offer them an **anecdote**.	Give them a **problem** to consider.	Ask them a **rhetorical question**.	Tell them an interesting / surprising **fact**.
Method	Tell a short story related to your topic about a real incident or person.	Ask the audience how they would solve a particular problem that is related to your topic.	Ask the audience to consider or reconsider a specific point that is relevant to your topic.	Direct the audience's thinking by using powerful facts / statistics / etc. that support your points.

MONOLOG

Fill in the blanks. Listen and check. `Track 3-04`

comprehend	fact	market	obtain

Good afternoon, everyone. Let me just begin by introducing myself. My name is Horatio Strong, and my position is in the sales department.

As you can tell from the title of my presentation, the topic I would like to look at today is methods to _____ customer feedback about products through the use of big data. By the end of my presentation, you'll _____ not only why obtaining feedback via big data is useful but also why it'll soon be absolutely necessary to compete in the _____. I've divided my talk today into three parts. First, I'll give some background information on big data. Second, we'll take a look at how to obtain big data, and third, we'll discuss how to examine it.

Before I get into my first point, let me get started by telling you an amazing _____. Did you know that last year more than 90% of our customers used a smartphone to purchase our products? That's up over 25% from just a year ago.

VOCABULARY

Match the words that have the same meaning.

1. roughly •
2. outline •
3. convince •
4. topic •
5. pertinent •

• a. persuade
• b. relevant
• c. about
• d. subject
• e. define

PRACTICE

Fill in the blanks with the correct word or phrase.

split	topic	take a look at	begin	examine

1. Good afternoon. Let me _____ by introducing myself.

2. The _____ I want to focus on today is big data and customer feedback.

3. I have _____ my talk today into three parts.

4. First, we will _____ some background information on big data.

5. Then we will talk about how to _____ these data.

Learning Objectives

- To learn vocabulary for linking parts of a presentation
- To use linking phrases to signal shifts in topic / section
- To understand how to refer to different sections

WARM-UP

1. Why is it important to signal the end of a section in a presentation?
2. What are some ways to signal the beginning of a new section?
3. What are some different ways to ask the audience to recall information?

Vocabulary

NOUNS
idea
point
profits
thoughts

VERBS
come back to
complete
deal with
digress
explore
relate
return
sequence
signal
share
shift
turn to

ADJECTIVES
final

ADVERBS
additionally

PREPOSITIONS
concerning
despite

Linking Parts of a Presentation — Useful Phrases

Sequencing ideas

- First / Second / Third / Then / Next / Finally...
- The first / second / third / final point is...

Signaling the end of a section

- This brings me to the end of my first / second / third point.
- I think that's all I wanted to say about...

Opening a new section

- In this part of my presentation, I'd like to shift attention toward...
- Let's now turn to the next part of my presentation...

Exploring a list of points

- In terms of... / Regarding... / In relation to...
- Concerning... / With respect to... / As it relates to...

Adding ideas

- Additionally,... / In addition to this,... / Moreover,... / Let's digress to...
- However,... / Despite this,...

Going back

- Let me now return / come back to...
- As I mentioned / stated / shared / explained earlier,...

Summarizing

- So, let me summarize what we've looked at up to this point.
- Alright, I'd like to sum up the main thoughts I've gone through so far.

Useful Expressions with "As"	As you all know,...	As I've previously explained,...	As I will explain to you in a moment,...	As you can clearly see,...

MONOLOG

Fill in the blanks. Listen and check. `Track 3-05`

thoughts	final	turn to	As I will explain to you in a moment

> In terms of energy, green energy is the future not only for businesses but also for countries around the world. So, as you can clearly see, there is a real need to move toward renewables. Alright everyone, this brings me to the end of my second point.
>
> _____, we can help your company move toward green energy. But before I move on to my _____ point, I want to _____ some examples of how we have already helped businesses across a wide range of industries make that change. So let's take a moment to shift our _____ to some of our customers right now. Here is a list of some of the biggest companies we have completed successful projects with. With respect to how quickly we completed these projects, here are those numbers. Additionally, you can see that our clients actually saw their profits increase after moving away from carbon-based energy sources.
>
> So, with that in mind, let's now return to the main discussion.

VOCABULARY

Circle the word that does not belong in each group.

1. additionally   however   furthermore   moreover
2. despite   moreover   regardless of   in spite of
3. explore   discuss   talk about   postpone
4. point   idea   move   thought
5. concerning   with respect to   as you know   as it relates to

PRACTICE

Match each phrase with the correct signposting function.

1. In terms of energy, green energy is the future. •
2. This brings me to the end of my second point. •
3. Additionally, you can see that... •
4. In the third part of my presentation, I'd like to • talk about how we can help your company.
5. So, with that in mind, let's now return to • the main discussion.

- a. going back
- b. exploring a list of points
- c. opening a new section
- d. signaling the end of a section
- e. adding ideas

→ *Activity File* page 116

Learning Objectives

- To learn vocabulary for highlighting specific parts of a presentation

- To use a range of phrases to emphasize key points

- To practice using intensifiers with positive and negative expressions

WARM-UP

1. What are some ways to emphasize a particular point?
2. What are some of the reasons to highlight a particular point?
3. How often do you tend to emphasize your ideas and opinions?

Vocabulary

NOUNS
disaster
improvement
option
reality
repetition
solution

VERBS
achieve
articulate
contrast
emphasize
reiterate
stress

ADJECTIVES
absolute
brilliant
dramatic
outstanding
remarkable

ADVERBS
basically
simply
totally

Highlighting & Emphasizing — Useful Phrases

Focusing
- I'd like to emphasize / stress...
- I should reiterate / repeat...
- It is critical / essential to understand...

Articulating with "What"
- What we can't do is...
- What I'd like to do is...
- What we have been able to achieve is...

Using repetition
- It is very, very important we choose the right option.
- We need to do something, and we need to do it now.

Simplifying
- Let me be clear... / Basically,... / To put it simply,... / In other words,...

Using dramatic language
- A total / absolute / complete disaster
- A great / outstanding / remarkable success / improvement
- Totally unacceptable / Quite brilliant

Contrasting
- Actually,... / In fact,... / In reality,... / The truth is that...

Biz Tip
Emphasize, highlight, and strengthen your points by using the appropriate intensifiers.

Form	positive	negative
Intensifiers	rather	at all
Example	It is **rather** remarkable.	It is not remarkable **at all**.

MONOLOG

Fill in the blanks. Listen and check. [Track 3-06]

rather	reiterate	contrast	achieve

Now let me move into the next part of my presentation, which is about how we collect and analyze feedback from our customers. We can _____ the results from the company's product feedback through traditional means, such as questionnaires and surveys, with the results I found by analyzing big data. When we do contrast them, there is a _____ remarkable difference in the quality of feedback from these two methods. So, let me be clear: I think analyzing big data is better and will allow us to make more improvements with our products and services. But let me _____ that it's very, very critical to be open to hearing client feedback from the traditional methods as well. It really depends on how customers prefer to give us feedback. So it's not as if traditional customer feedback has no place at all anymore. Therefore, I think what we can do is figure out the best way to use both types of feedback to _____ the best results.

VOCABULARY

Match each word with the correct meaning.

1. disaster •
2. articulate •
3. brilliant •
4. dramatic •
5. simply •

• a. give a clear explanation of something
• b. unusually good, smart, or positive
• c. easily
• d. striking in appearance, characteristics, or effect
• e. an event that brings a large amount of damage, loss, or destruction

PRACTICE

Fill in the blanks with the correct word.

improvements	options	absolute	emphasize	remarkable

1. I would like to _____ the importance of collecting feedback through a variety of channels.

2. Analyzing feedback will help us to make _____ to our products.

3. The difference between the two types of feedback is pretty _____.

4. We have several _____ as to how we can collect this feedback.

5. Having these multiple feedback channels is an _____ necessity for us.

→ *Activity File* page 116

07 Engaging Your Audience

Learning Objectives

- To learn vocabulary for addressing an audience
- To use a range of phrases to engage an audience
- To understand techniques for addressing the audience

Vocabulary

NOUNS

clarification
experiment
point of view
rapport
relationship
sense
statistics

VERBS

acknowledge
afford
dwell
ignore
lead to
realize

ADJECTIVES

diplomatic
directed
satisfied
sufficient
valuable

ADVERBS

honestly
sincerely

WARM-UP

1. Why is it important to engage your audience?
2. What are some different ways to engage an audience?
3. When should you change the methods of engagement you use?

Engaging Your Audience — Useful Phrases

Asking questions

Rhetorical questions

- Are we satisfied with this product?
- Is this company sincerely acknowledging its problems?
- Can we afford to ignore this problem?

Directed questions

- George, I know you have a lot of valuable experience. Could you comment?
- Perhaps I can ask Peter to answer that question. Peter?
- I'd like to try a thought experiment. Imagine...
- Could you offer your point of view...?
- Can I ask for a show of hands?
- How many of you...?
- How many people here have ever...?

Clarification questions

- Is that sufficient?
- Are there any questions about that?
- Does that make sense?

Creating rapport and being diplomatic

- We need to think honestly about what this will lead to.
- We don't need to dwell on this.
- I know what you are thinking.
- I'm sure everyone in this room has...
- I'm sure you don't need me to tell you that...
- I realize you all know...

> **Biz Tip**
>
> *Try to use inclusive language like "we," "us," and "our" instead of "I," "me," and "my."*

Form	subject pronouns	object pronouns	possessive pronouns
Inclusive	we	us	our
Example	**We** can achieve a lot.	It will be a benefit to **us**.	It's in **our** mutual interest.

DIALOG

Fill in the blanks. Listen and check. `Track 3-07`

	us	rapport	honestly	diplomatic

Angela: Developing a _____ with the client is critical. From your point of view, Mark, has developing a rapport with clients led to any significant changes in the way you deal with them?

Mark: I think it has made me more _____ in dealing with complaints.

Angela: That's an excellent point. Let me see a show of hands of the number of people here who have felt lost when dealing with complaints? Lots of _____. I tended to feel that way that too. That was because my expectation was that I had to defend the product. Now, I acknowledge the complaint as a situation where the client is offering us valuable feedback. Can we afford to ignore this kind of feedback from our clients? Absolutely not! That is why we need to sincerely build a good relationship with our customers. If we can acknowledge when we're wrong, and try to fix the problem, then our customers will realize that we're dealing with them _____. Consequently, they will be willing to continue being our customers and have a stronger relationship with us.

VOCABULARY

Match the words that have the same meaning.

1. sincerely •   • a. acceptable

2. statistics •   • b. truly

3. valuable •   • c. result in

4. sufficient •   • d. numbers

5. lead to •   • e. helpful

PRACTICE

Match each sentence with the word or phrase that best completes it.

1. How has developing a ___ with your clients helped you? •   • a. diplomatic

2. It's better to ___ complaints than try to ignore them. •   • b. point of view

3. We have to be ___ when dealing with client complaints. •   • c. sincerely

4. Dealing with a client honestly and ___ is the key to maintaining a long-term relationship. •   • d. rapport

5. You must always consider the other party's ___. •   • e. acknowledge

→ *Activity File* page 117

08 Visuals

Learning Objectives

- To learn vocabulary related to visuals
- To use a range of vocabulary to describe charts
- To practice language that can be used with visuals

WARM-UP

1. What types of visuals can be used in a presentation?
2. Why are visuals helpful to use during a presentation?
3. What language is helpful to use with visuals?

Vocabulary

NOUNS

chart
graph
peak
plateau
recovery
volatility

VERBS

decrease
fall
increase
plummet
regress
rocket
slump
suffer
worsen

ADJECTIVES

stable
steady

ADVERBS

gradually
rapidly
slightly

Visuals — Useful Language

Describing changes

to go up / to be up by	to go down / to be down by
to increase / an increase of	to decrease / a decrease of
to rise / a rise of	to fall / a fall of
to grow / a growth of	to shrink / a decline of
to improve / an improvement	to regress / a regression
to recover / a recovery	to suffer / a loss
to (sky)rocket / shoot up	to plummet / sink / slump
to remain stable	to level out / off
to plateau / to hit a ceiling	to reach / hit a peak / to peak

Describing pace of changes

- rapidly / rapid
- steadily / steady
- gradually / gradual
- slowly / slow
- V-shaped / U-shaped / W-shaped
- volatile / volatility

Biz Tip

Use intensifiers with visuals to clearly describe the degree of change.

Intensifiers	dramatic extreme	significant very + (adj.)	moderate pretty + (adj.)	slight somewhat of
	dramatically extremely	significantly very + (adv.)	moderately pretty + (adv.)	slightly somewhat
Level of Strength	stronger ⟵		⟶ less strong	

MONOLOG

Fill in the blanks. Listen and check. `Track 3-08`

graph	stable	significant	volatility

As you can see on this _____, there was a lot of _____ in terms of our sales figures this year.

We began the year very strongly, with year-on-year sales skyrocketing by 78%. This was mainly due to our overseas expansion. However, due to the unexpected and _____ increase in shipping and transportation costs, we had to scale back our expansion. This is reflected in this slide. What you're looking at here are two charts that compare our first quarter and second quarter international sales. As you can see, they shrank dramatically.

However, in the third quarter, the shipping and transportation costs gradually leveled out, and we were able to press on with our global expansion. That is reflected in this last chart here, which shows a V-shaped recovery of our overseas sales starting in the third quarter. We're hoping that the shipping costs will remain _____, and that we can continue to moderately grow our international sales to finish out the rest of this year.

VOCABULARY

Match the words that have the opposite meaning.

1. increase •   • a. slowly
2. rocket •   • b. decrease
3. rapidly •   • c. plummet
4. steady •   • d. regress
5. improve •   • e. volatile

PRACTICE

Match each sentence with the word that best completes it.

1. We began the year very strongly with year-on-year sales ____ by 78%. •   • a. rocketing

2. What you're looking at here are two ____ that compare our first quarter and second quarter international sales. •   • b. steadily

3. As you can see, they ____ dramatically. •   • c. charts

4. This shows a V-shaped ____ of our overseas sales starting in the third quarter. •   • d. recovery

5. We hope we can ____ grow our international sales. •   • e. shrank

→ *Activity File* page 117

09 Body Language & Persuasion

Learning Objectives

- To learn vocabulary that describes body language
- To use a range of persuasive phrases / structures
- To practice emotive language that complements body language

Vocabulary

NOUNS

advantage
appearance
attire
boredom
disadvantage
gesture
individual
posture
proposal
stance

VERBS

augment
maintain
prevent
suggest

ADJECTIVES

comfortable
enormous
enthusiastic
persuasive
risky
superior

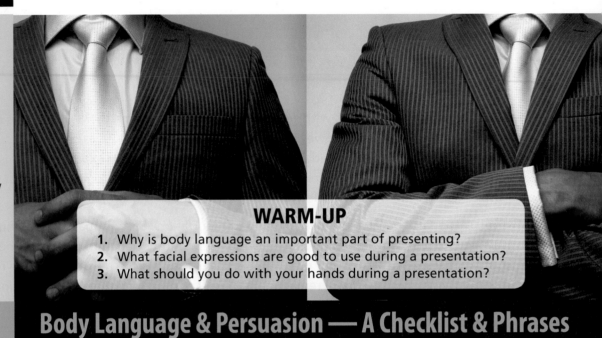

WARM-UP

1. Why is body language an important part of presenting?
2. What facial expressions are good to use during a presentation?
3. What should you do with your hands during a presentation?

Body Language & Persuasion — A Checklist & Phrases

Facial expression, body language, and attire

- ☐ Match your appearance to the atmosphere and expectations.
- ☐ Maintain eye contact with a few different individuals.
- ☐ Ensure that your facial expressions match and augment your message.
- ☐ Move around the room to show confidence and prevent boredom.
- ☐ Use hand gestures to direct attention and create impact.
- ☐ Establish a confident yet comfortable posture and stance.
- ☐ Create a positive attitude—be relaxed and enthusiastic.
- ☐ Give lists of three things and count with your fingers.

Persuasive language

- I suggest that we...
- My suggestion is that we...
- I recommend that we...
- My recommendation is that we...
- I propose that we...
- My proposal is that we...
- The difference between... and... is enormous.
- What are the advantages and disadvantages of...?
- On the one hand... / On the other hand...
- This is far superior to / better than...
- We have no choice.
- If we don't... then we will see...
- Either we... or...
- Instead of..., we could...

> **Biz Tip**
>
> *Strongly emphasize emotive language and gesture with your hands in order to maximize persuasiveness.*

Emotive Language	This is like **playing with fire**.	This will cause a **huge mess**.	This is an **absolute must**.	We might **never hear the end of this**.
Neutral Language	It is **risky**.	This may be a **problem**.	We **require** this.	Some folks might **complain**.

DIALOG

Fill in the blanks. Listen and check. `Track 3-09`

proposal	absolute must	posture	risky

David: Thank you for helping me prepare for my presentation. So, after listening to my _____, what do you think?

Elaine: I think you made a very interesting proposal during your presentation.

David: Thanks. I think this new idea has a lot of advantages.

Elaine: Right. I could tell that you're very enthusiastic about it.

David: I just hope I can convince the managers. It's a little _____, you know?

Elaine: Yeah, it is. I suggest improving your _____ and stance during the presentation a bit in order to be more persuasive.

David: Oh, right. I have bad posture, but if I stand a little straighter, it will communicate more confidence in the proposal. What about my facial expression and gestures?

Elaine: You smiled a lot while you were talking about the proposal, which is good. But you kept smiling while you were talking about the risks, which was a little strange. Your facial expression didn't match what you were talking about.

David: Oh, right. Appropriate facial expressions are an _____. Thank you for all the feedback. I'm feeling even more confident now.

VOCABULARY

Match each word with the correct meaning.

1. appearance •
2. individual •
3. attire •
4. augment •
5. superior •

• a. help or improve something by adding to it
• b. the way a person or thing looks
• c. a person
• d. of higher effectiveness, importance, quality, or quantity
• e. a clothing outfit, usually carefully selected and worn for a specific purpose

PRACTICE

Choose the best word to complete each sentence.

1. I think the proposal is good because it has a lot of _____.
   a. advantages   b. disadvantages   c. individuals   d. gestures

2. You seem very _____ about this idea.
   a. enthusiastic   b. superior   c. risky   d. enormous

3. You can improve your posture and _____.
   a. disadvantage   b. advantage   c. stance   d. boredom

4. I think by looking more confident you can be more _____.
   a. risky   b. persuasive   c. enormous   d. superior

5. How were my facial expressions and _____?
   a. individuals   b. proposals   c. disadvantages   d. gestures

→ *Activity File* page 118

10 Communication Styles

WARM-UP

1. What are some different styles of communication?
2. What style of communication do you think is most comfortable for you?
3. Why is it important to adjust your communication style to your audience?

Vocabulary

NOUNS

approach
catastrophe
moment
strength
worry

VERBS

agree
cause
overstate
perceive
prefer

ADJECTIVES

balanced
detached
emphatic
in-depth
involved
organic
slight
systematic

ADVERBS

emotionally
naturally

Communication Styles — Useful Phrases

Understand how you naturally communicate with others so that you can try to improve your presentation skills by having a balanced approach.

Formal vs. Informal: Do you prefer a formal or informal tone?

On behalf of... may I welcome you to...	vs.	Thanks for coming.
We will acquire the company soon.	vs.	We'll buy them out soon.
We perceive it differently.	vs.	We have a different point of view.

Closed vs. Open: Do you state facts or ask and discuss questions?

The facts tell us that...	vs.	After seeing the facts, do you agree that...?
I believe that...	vs.	Do you think that...?
We should find a way to...	vs.	Shouldn't we find a way to...?

Emphatic vs. Relaxed: How much do you tend to overstate things?

This is a really big problem.	vs.	This is a slight worry.
This is a catastrophe.	vs.	This may cause a problem.
I'm convinced...	vs.	I tend to think that...

Involved vs. Detached: Do you engage emotionally or remain detached?

I think...	vs.	It is thought...
I arranged it.	vs.	It was arranged.
We'll look at this in a moment.	vs.	This will be looked at in a moment.

> **Biz Tip**
>
> *Use "just" as a modifier to be more persuasive.*

Modifiers	Sometimes **just** can strengthen what you say (similar to "seriously" or "very")	Sometimes **just** can soften what you say. (similar to "only" or "simply")
Example	This is **just** a catastrophe.	This is **just** a slight worry.

MONOLOG

Fill in the blanks. Listen and check. `Track 3-10`

catastrophe	overstate	just	perceive

This brings me to my last point. I don't want to _____ the problem or seem like I'm thinking about this too emotionally. However, I've shown you the facts, and I do think that there is a real worry here. I believe it could lead to a _____ if we just continue to do business as usual. There is real cause for concern and serious danger.

So, that is why we need to change our approach. Otherwise, we'll never improve our performance, and sales could _____ plummet by next year. On the other hand, if we utilize the new approach I've outlined in a systematic way, our sales should rocket by early next year.

This is how I _____ the problem and the solution. Naturally, though, I would like your feedback on this idea. We need a balanced approach to this, and we need an in-depth analysis of the strengths and weaknesses of this idea before we apply it.

VOCABULARY

Match the words that have the same meaning.

1. prefer •
2. in-depth •
3. approach •
4. cause •
5. emphatic •

• a. detailed
• b. method
• c. strong
• d. like
• e. create

PRACTICE

Fill in the blanks with the correct word.

emotionally	agree	systematic	worry	Naturally

1. I don't want to seem like I'm thinking about this too _____.

2. As you can see, there is a real _____ here.

3. I have outlined a new plan in a _____ way.

4. _____, I would like to hear your opinions about my plan.

5. I hope you all _____ with me that there is a problem here.

→ Activity File page 118

11 Closing a Presentation

Learning Objectives

- To learn vocabulary for summarizing points
- To use a range of phrases to close a presentation
- To learn a variety of strategies for concluding a presentation

WARM-UP

1. What is the best way to end a presentation?
2. What information should you give at the end of a presentation?
3. How much time should you leave for questions?

Vocabulary

NOUNS

demand
opportunity
partnership
target

VERBS

advise
appoint
appreciate
approach
expand
forge
formulate
leave
located
recommend
sum up

ADJECTIVES

overseas
wonderful

ADVERBS

attentively
briefly
therefore

Closing a Presentation — Useful Phrases

Signaling the end

- OK. That brings me to the end of my presentation.
- Right. That covers everything I wanted to say about...
- So, we're approaching the end here.

Summarizing the main ideas

- To sum up then,... / If I could briefly summarize,...
- Before I finish, let me just go over...

Concluding

- To conclude, I'd like to say that... / I'd like to finish by saying... / In conclusion,...

Final recommendation

- It seems to me, then, that we should...
- I would therefore recommend / advise that...

Support

- I have prepared a handout which I will pass around.
- Here are my contact details in case you want to follow up.

Closing

- Thank you for listening so attentively. You've been wonderful.
- I appreciate the opportunity to talk with you today.

Inviting questions

- I'd be glad to answer any questions at this time. / So, are there any questions?

> **Biz Tip**
>
> *Choose your conclusion strategy based on the purpose of your presentation.*

Conclusion Strategy	call to action	quote a well-known individual	reiterate the main idea	tell a story
Example	So this is why we need to...	As... famously said,...	Recall what I said at the beginning of this talk.	Let me leave you with this story.

MONOLOG

Fill in the blanks. Listen and check. `Track 3-11`

forge	appoint	famously said	approaching

We're now _____ the end of this discussion on formulating a new sales
strategy for expanding our overseas business. Just to sum up the main points, we need to
_____ new and better partnerships with companies that are located in our target
markets, we need to make a strong push to boost our online presence, and we need to scale the
size of our sales staff so that our human resources match the demand. I'd like to conclude with
one final recommendation, which is that we _____ someone whose job it is to
ensure all of these objectives are met. I have a handout that I'll pass out to everyone with some
recommendations about how we might do this. Remember, if we want a different and better
result, we have to do things differently. As the late, great Steve Jobs _____,
"Think different." And with that, I'd like to thank you for listening so attentively. I'd be glad to
answer any questions you have at this time.

VOCABULARY

Circle the word that does not belong in each group.

1. opportunity   chance   opening   advice
2. expand   meet   grow   increase
3. wonderful   questionable   excellent   great
4. briefly   quickly   shortly   differently
5. formulate   build   hear   make

PRACTICE

Fill in the blanks with the correct word.

demand	overseas	partnerships	recommend	attentively

1. We've been discussing how to formulate a new sales strategy for our _____ business.

2. We need to create better _____ with companies in our target markets.

3. We also need to ensure our people can meet the _____.

4. Thank you for listening _____.

5. I'd like to _____ that we name someone to lead this effort.

Learning Objectives

- To learn vocabulary for handling questions
- To use a range of phrases to help understand questions
- To practice a range of skills related to responding to questions

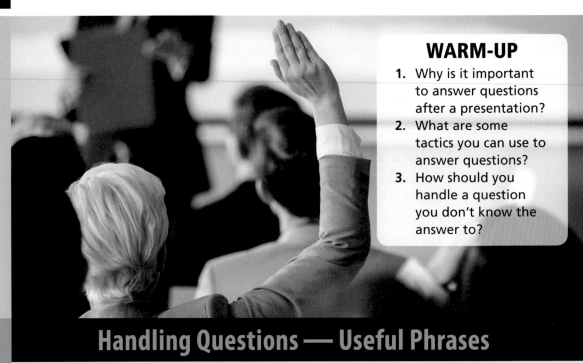

Vocabulary

NOUNS

area
criticism
degree
extent
field
liberty

VERBS

allow
make clear
mention
point out

ADJECTIVES

certain
complex
difficult
fair
glad
interesting

ADVERBS

beyond
correctly
fully
partially

Handling Questions — Useful Phrases

Positive response

- That's a good / difficult / complex / an interesting question.
- I'm glad someone asked that question. It allows me to say...

Check your answer

- Does that answer your question? / Is that OK?
- Is that clear? / Does that make it clear?

Clarify

- If I understand you correctly, you want to know...
- Sorry, I didn't fully follow / catch the question.
- In other words, you're asking...

Refer back

- As I mentioned in the first section / at the end of the second section,...
- Yes, as I pointed out / explained earlier,...

Accept criticism

- I accept that. / That's a fair point. / I agree with that.
- I partially agree. / I think to a certain degree / extent you're right.

Deflecting expertise

- Unfortunately, I'm the wrong person to answer that.
- That's not really my area / field, I'm afraid.

Rejecting the topic

- I'm afraid that question goes beyond the subject for today.
- I'm sorry but that's confidential. / I'm not at liberty to say.

> **Biz Tip**
>
> *"Let's discuss that after the presentation"* is a response that should be used as little as possible, but it can be used to help you avoid answering awkward or irrelevant questions when necessary.

Answering a Question with a Question	OK, let me ask you something / the same question / a question.	I can answer that by asking you a question.	Well, what's your opinion on that?

DIALOG

Fill in the blanks. Listen and check. `Track 3-12`

let me ask you	complex	beyond	allow

Jayne: I'd be glad to answer any questions you have now.

Wes: So, are you saying we should just put one person in charge of overseas expansion, or that we should create a whole new team?

Jayne: I guess I am saying both of those things. In other words, what I'm saying is we should appoint the right person to lead the overseas expansion and _____ them to have whatever they need to get the job done. That could include creating a whole new team. Does that make things clear?

Wes: It does, but that makes me wonder, would we be putting too much effort into this?

Jayne: Well, I think that is _____ my area of expertise, unfortunately. I think the HR team would probably be the right team to answer that. My main focus here today is to talk about the best place to expand our sales.

Wes: Right. That's fair. It's a _____ issue. But don't you think it's a little bit risky?

Jayne: I think to a certain extent you're right. But _____ a question. Isn't it risky if we do not expand our sales overseas? We could be missing an important chance.

VOCABULARY

Find the word in the vocabulary list with the same meaning and write it on the line.

1. freedom   _____

2. happy   _____

3. hard   _____

4. rightly   _____

5. completely   _____

PRACTICE

Correct the mistake in each of the following sentences.

1. In <u>another</u> words, I'm saying we should appoint the right person to lead the overseas expansion.

2. Does that <u>making</u> it clear?

3. I think to a <u>certainly</u> extent you're right.

4. Right. I think that's <u>fare</u>.

5. As I <u>mention</u> earlier, this is a complex issue.

13 Presentations in Different Cultures

Learning Objectives

- To learn vocabulary to help with cross-cultural presentations
- To recognize different cultural approaches to presentations
- To practice cross-cultural presentations

WARM-UP

1. Have you given a presentation to people from other cultures?
2. Have you listened to presentations by people from other countries?
3. What are some cross-cultural considerations that should be made?

Vocabulary

NOUNS

analysis
animation
dress code
factor
hierarchy
interaction
interruption
lack
personality
pocket
precision
sloppiness
spontaneity

VERBS

consider
contribute
favor

ADJECTIVES

negative
reserved
rigid
strict

Cross-Cultural Tips — A Database

When preparing a presentation, consider the following:

Communication factors

| **Animation:** Some audiences prefer a reserved style to enthusiasm. |
| **Human touch:** Some audiences like to see the presenter's personality. |
| **Interaction:** Some audiences simply want to listen and not contribute. |
| **Interruption:** Some audiences expect to be able to interrupt. |
| **Language:** Some audiences have varying English ability. |
| **Level of analysis:** Many audiences have in-depth specialist knowledge. |
| **Reading text:** Some audiences favor spontaneity over precision. |
| **Role of silence:** Some audiences do not view silence negatively. |

Social factors

| **Body & Face:** Some audiences expect a presenter to be dynamic. |
| **Business card:** Some audiences will request a business card. |
| **Dress:** Some audiences work in companies with strict dress codes. |
| **Eye contact:** Some audiences feel uncomfortable without eye contact. |
| **Formality:** Some audiences see informality as a lack of professionalism. |
| **Hands:** Some audiences view hands in pockets as sloppiness. |
| **Hierarchy:** Most audiences respect social and corporate hierarchies. |
| **Punctuality:** Most audiences expect punctuality. |
| **Systematic:** Some audiences prefer a rigid structure and style. |

> **Biz Tip**
>
> *You can skillfully navigate cross-cultural situations by using these useful phrases to clarify expectations, differences, and a lack of cultural knowledge.*

Useful Phrases	In…, we / they / it…	Is it alright if I…?	I didn't know…
Examples	**In** Asia, **it** is common to exchange business cards at the first meeting.	**Is it alright if I** call you by your first name?	**I didn't know** that you shouldn't do that.

DIALOG

Fill in the blanks. Listen and check. Track 3-13

contribute	consider	rigid	in some Asian cultures

Tiffany: We'll need to get used to giving presentations to audiences from a variety of different cultures since we are going to be expanding overseas.

Francisco: That's a good point. I'm sure there are a lot of factors to _____. Have you thought about giving a workshop on presentations?

Tiffany: Yes. In fact, I've been thinking about asking Brittany to help with that. She used to work for a company that did a lot of business all over the world. Maybe she could _____ her experience to help us make some training materials.

Francisco: That's a great idea. There are so many things we need to think about. For example, I heard that _____, it can be seen as rude to have your hand in your pocket while talking to other professionals. It's that kind of little thing that can distract from the message of the presentation and give us a negative image.

Tiffany: Right. And, on the other hand, we don't want to appear too _____ and strict.

Francisco: Yeah, that might make us look like we have a lack of personality. We need to find the right balance of professionalism and animation. We want to appear reserved, capable of precision, and still enjoyable to do business with.

VOCABULARY

Match each word with the correct meaning.

1. animation •
2. dress code •
3. hierarchy •
4. sloppiness •
5. spontaneity •

• a. a set of rules about what clothing may and may not be worn at a particular place
• b. a system in which people or things are placed in levels with different positions of authority and importance
• c. the level of liveliness and excitement
• d. the tendency to do things in a sudden way and without a lot of thought or planning
• e. not careful or organized

PRACTICE

Match each sentence with the word that best completes it.

1. In some cultures, it can be seen as rude to have your hand in your ____ while talking to other professionals. •
2. Cultural misunderstandings can distract from the presentation and give us a ____ image. •
3. We also don't want to appear too ____ and rigid. •
4. We don't want to show a ____ of personality. •
5. We want to appear ____, yet still enjoyable to do business with. •

• a. negative
• b. lack
• c. strict
• d. pocket
• e. reserved

→ *Activity File* page 120

14. Business Tips for Presenting

- To review key vocabulary for presentations
- To recognize best practices for presentations
- To practice & review structures & useful language for presentations

WARM-UP

1. What do you need to prepare for a successful presentation?
2. How can you signal to the audience that a change in focus is coming?
3. What do you need to consider along with the contents of the presentation?

Vocabulary

NOUNS
audio
factor
handout
idea
mannerisms
podium
point
section
talk
temperature

VERBS
conclude
cover
emphasize
ignore
outline
recommend
summarize

ADJECTIVES
dramatic

ADVERBS
fully
honestly

Business Tips for Presenting — Dos & Don'ts

		Do	Don't
Preparing		identify the purpose, objective, and presentation type	use language, ideas, or examples that don't fit your presentation type
		ensure the audio, podium, temperature, etc., are ready	assume that the equipment you need and environment you want will be prepared
Starting		make an impact with your mannerisms, handouts, etc.	ignore factors such as visuals, body language, etc.
		use the WISE OWL process to begin your presentation	forget to use a hook after doing a WISE OWL intro
Presenting		outline your ideas and the sections of your talk	emphasize minor points, use overly dramatic words, etc.
		use signposting to signal as you move from one topic to the next	forget to summarize a point you cover before moving to the next point
Concluding		signal the end of the presentation and recommend what should be done	go past the allotted amount of time
		allow and answer questions as completely, fully, and honestly as you can	handle all questions the same way

Section	introduction	opening	main contents	visuals	conclusion	questions
Strategies & Phrases	WISE OWL	hook	This brings me to my main / next point...	Let's take a look at this...	So that concludes...	Are there any questions?

DIALOG

Fill in the blanks. Listen and check. `Track 3-14`

So that concludes	talk	mannerisms	point

Jia: _____ my list of top tips for giving a successful presentation. Do you guys have any questions?

Vince: Yes, I do. How can we figure out if we have appropriate _____, body language, facial expressions, gestures, and so on?

Jia: I'm glad you asked that. So, first of all, you should find out what's appropriate for the culture you're doing the presentation for. And that goes for commercial as well as for national culture. Some industries are more strict and rigid than others.

Vince: OK. Good _____. But you only partially answered my question.

Jia: Oh, right. Sorry. So some good ways to check and practice your mannerisms are to present in front of a mirror, in front of a friend, or to record yourself with your phone and then watch it back.

Vince: What about telling jokes or anecdotes during a presentation? Is that OK?

Jia: I think jokes are best avoided. But a good anecdote could be helpful for getting your point across. So, for example, if it helps introduce your _____, I think an anecdote is fine.

VOCABULARY

Match each word with the correct meaning.

1. audio •
2. handout •
3. emphasize •
4. ignore •
5. honestly •

• a. truthfully
• b. focus on
• c. information paper
• d. forget
• e. sound

PRACTICE

Fill in the blanks with the correct word.

talk	idea	recommend	summarizing	covers

1. So that _____ all the best tips I can give you on how to give a presentation.

2. Do you have any questions about my _____?

3. I _____ that you avoid jokes.

4. Anecdotes can work well to help explain an _____ in your presentation.

5. Thank you for _____ all of your best tips on how to give a successful presentation.

CASE STUDY

CHAPTER 03: English for Presentations
Risk Management Portfolio: Risk vs. Reward

Part Ⓐ Background

All companies need to manage risk. Different types of businesses have different levels of built-in risk. For example, a company with a complex supply chain is exposed to more risk factors and can suffer when a shock hits one of its suppliers. Companies also intentionally take measured risks when they think it could have a positive result, such as more profits or faster growth. Depending on internal conditions within the company, and external economic conditions, a company's approach to risk can change. For example, when conditions are seen as relatively safe, stable, and certain, many companies choose an aggressive risk management portfolio. In contrast, when conditions are bad, companies want less risk. By taking fewer risks, companies can protect themselves, but the possibility of reward is also smaller.

Part Ⓑ Task

Think about the company you currently work for, or a company you would like to work for. Research and brainstorm what some of the internal and external risk factors are, and then explore where the potential areas for growth, profits, and other rewards are. Write your considerations in the chart below.

Risk-Reward Analysis Profile

Risk Factors	Reward Potential
Internal – *rising operating costs*	– *overseas growth potential*
External – *global recession*	

Brainstorm: Based on the risk-reward analysis, choose a risk management portfolio for your company for the next three years. Consider the pros and cons of each strategy, then choose one.

Future 3-Year Risk Management Strategy

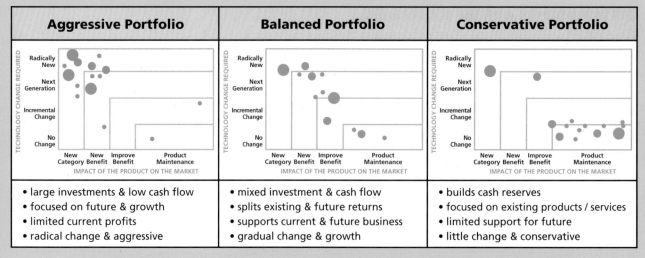

Aggressive Portfolio	Balanced Portfolio	Conservative Portfolio
• large investments & low cash flow • focused on future & growth • limited current profits • radical change & aggressive	• mixed investment & cash flow • splits existing & future returns • supports current & future business • gradual change & growth	• builds cash reserves • focused on existing products / services • limited support for future • little change & conservative

Part C Preparation

Imagine you will give a presentation to high level managers in your company about which risk management strategy is best to follow. Choose one type of presentation you think will work best for you to communicate the risk management strategy you selected.

Tip Review the checklist on p. 72.

Presentation Type

☐ Inform the audience	☐ Persuade the audience	☐ Sell something to the audience	☐ Train the audience

Main Idea	Supporting Points, Data, and Examples
Our company should have a(n) _____ risk management portfolio	

Part D Write a Skeleton Presentation

With a clear understanding of the risk-reward picture of your company, plan a presentation for the managers in your company.

Tip Review the process on p. 76.

1. WISE Intro (Do all 4)		2. OWL Intro (Do all 3)		3. Hook (Choose 1)	
Welcome the audience		Outline the structure		An anecdote	
Introduce yourself		When each part will come		A problem to think about	
Say what the topic is				A rhetorical question	
Explain why the audience will be interested		Link to the start		An interesting fact	

Part E Finalize and Do Your Presentation

Add details, figures, examples, etc., to finalize your presentation. Practice the presentation and then do it in front of the class.

ACTIVITY FILE

🎧 Scan for Audio

Scenario:

You are the head of the business development division for a large corporation. You are working with a junior colleague to prepare a conference call with an overseas business partner. Write an email with a checklist of tasks you want the junior colleague to prepare before the conference call.

Tip *Look at the checklist on p. 6 for an example.*

New message   — ⤢ ✕

To
_____

Subject
_____

Send   A 📎 🔗 ☺ 🖼   ⋮ 🗑

Scenario:

You work for the HR department at a company that is going to start to have employees work from home. Make a best practices guide for employees about how to use Zoom for work-related discussions. Review the steps and use the language learned in the lesson to write the guide.

Create an account	*Be sure to use a professional, secure email address: not a private one.*
Schedule the call	
Share the call link	
Make the call	
Use the host tools	

Scenario:

Role-play a call between a caller who works for an advertising company and an executive assistant who works at a company called KS Games. Work with a partner, choose a role, and use the language learned in the lesson to fill in the tables below.

Role A: Executive Assistant Take the call and attempt to transfer the call. Explain that the head of marketing at your company is on vacation.		**Role B: Caller** You work for an advertising company and you want to speak to the head of the marketing team at KS Games to help advertise their new game.	
Greet and identify	*Good morning, KS Games. My name is...*	Greet and identify	*Good morning. My name is...*
Ask about the purpose		Explain the purpose	
Confirm information and connect		Confirm information	
Apology / No connection		Ask to leave message	

Scenario:

The head of sales is messaging a member of the accounting team to get information about changes to the customer billing process. The sales team needs to know who will pay for domestic and international shipping fees—the company or the customer. Complete the conversation below.

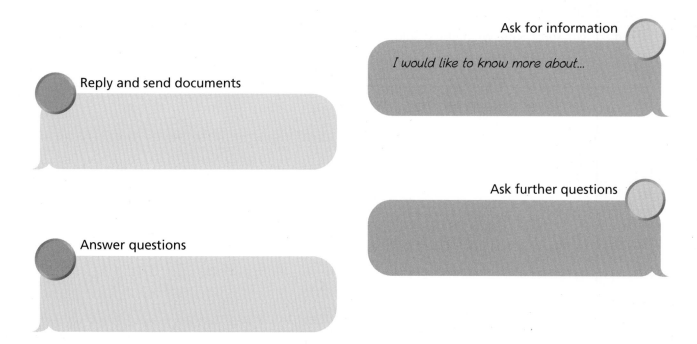

Ask for information

I would like to know more about...

Reply and send documents

Ask further questions

Answer questions

Scenario:

Listen to a conversation between a caller and a customer service representative. Take down a message with the caller's information.

Name and company	_____ *from Pacifica Health Services Limited.*
Message	
Time and date	
Contact Details	

Scenario:

A customer is calling to discuss billing for an existing order and to request information about a new product. Read the call transcript. Rewrite the conversation so it is structured more effectively. Add and remove details as appropriate.

Tip (*Look at the dialog on p. 17 for an example.*)

Jack:	I'm calling to ask about the billing for an order.
Fred:	Would it be alright if we put a pin in that?
Jack:	Well, sure. But could I ask why?
Fred:	The manager for that is out on business. She will be back on the 15th.
Jack:	Alright, no problem. I'll call back then.
Fred:	OK, thank you. Goodbye.
Jack:	Oh, actually there was one other reason why I called.
Fred:	Oh, sorry. Sure, what else would you like to discuss?
Jack:	I also need information about a new product. Sorry, I should've mentioned at the start.

Jack:	*I'm calling to discuss two things. First....*

Scenario:

Role-play a call between two business associates. Use appropriate words and phrases to complete the information exchange.

Tip *Look at the dialog on p. 19 for an example. And review spelling out names on p. 14.*

Role A: Fill in the blanks only for your role. Read the dialog with Person B, and write the answers they give.

Role B: Fill in the blanks only for your role. Read the dialog with Person A, and write the answers they give.

A:	Could you give Sam a message for me when he gets in? Are you ready?
B:	Yes, please go ahead.
A:	His sister Myra is arriving tonight, but I'm busy at work.
B:	Pardon? Could you _____?
A:	That's -M as in _____, -Y as in _____, -R as in _____, -A as in _____.
B:	She's on the 7:50 flight from Denver.
A:	Sorry, _____ breaking up. _____ 7:15?
B:	No, fifty. Five-zero. From Denver. _____ critical _____ message.
A:	Just to make sure there are not any *mistakes*, can you _____ to me, please?

Scenario:

Read the difficulties below. Identify the type of difficulty. Then work with a partner and brainstorm what you would say or do in response. Write down your answers and practice saying them.

Identify the problem	1. The other side keeps breaking up, and it's difficult to hear what they are saying. ⓐ general ⓑ device ⓒ sound ⓓ wrong number
Respond	_____ _____
Identify the problem	2. Someone calls you asking for a person you've never heard of. ⓐ network ⓑ sound ⓒ device ⓓ wrong number
Respond	*Sorry, there's no one here by that name. I think...* _____

Scenario:
Listen to a voice message and plan a return call. Include questions, confirmation of details, etc.

Your name and company	
Reason for call	
Thanking	
Returning to a previous subject	

Chapter 1 **Lesson 10: Activity, pages 24–25**

Scenario:
Role-play making lunch arrangements with a business associate. Work with a partner, choose a role, and use the language learned in the lesson to figure out if lunch will be possible today. If so, schedule the lunch. If not, schedule lunch for another day. Write your conversation below.

Role A: Director of Sales Schedule	Role B: Marketing Manager Schedule
Team meeting: 9:00 to 11:00.	Marketing seminar: 9:00 to 10:45.
International client call: 11:00 to 13:00.	Conference call: 10:45 to 11:30.
Sales call with a new customer: 14:00 to 16:00.	Meeting with online advertisers: 13:00 to 16:00.
Return to office, enter sales data: 16:00 to 18:00.	Ad blog updates: 16:00 to 18:00.

A:	*So, we are supposed to have that lunch meeting today. What is your schedule like?*
B:	
A:	
B:	
A:	
B:	
A:	
B:	

Scenario:

Role-play complaining and responding to a complaint. Work with a partner, choose a role, and use the language learned in the lesson. Write your conversation below.

Role A: Customer Service Representative	Role B: Customer
Take the customer's complaint and respond appropriately to the situation. Your records show that the customer ordered 30 soccer balls for their sports store.	Call and complain that you didn't receive the 300 soccer balls that you ordered for your sports store.

A:	*Hello, this TYJ Sports Equipment. I'm a customer service representative, and my name is _____. How can I assist you today?*
B:	
A:	
B:	
A:	
B:	
A:	
B:	

Scenario:

Listen to the other party in the two phone calls. Identify the function of what they are saying. Then choose the most appropriate way to respond. Write down how you want to respond. After that, work with a partner. Compare answers and practice saying them.

Identify the function	1. ⓐ closing the call ⓑ promising action ⓒ thanking ⓓ ending on a high note
Respond	_____ _____
Identify the function	2. ⓐ promising action ⓑ thanking ⓒ ending on a high note ⓓ saying goodbye
Respond	_____ _____

Scenario:

Complete a discussion about the most appropriate strategy for calling an overseas client with appropriate words and phrases. Choose a role and practice the conversation with a partner. Switch roles and practice again.

A:	I'm a little worried about calling Mr. Svenson in Sweden. I don't know anything about Swedish culture. Do you have any suggestions?
B:	Well, I've heard they like _____, so make sure to be on time.
A:	Right. Actually, now that you mention it, I do remember hearing that before too. What about directness? A lot of Americans tend to be very direct, but some other cultures find that a little rude or aggressive.
B:	Hmm. Well, I think that directness is probably a similarity they have with us. I think they _____ that because they think it shows honesty.
A:	Alright. Well, I want to make a good impression. Gaining his _____ is important, but what about using _____? Is it OK to make jokes?
B:	Well, I guess that depends on each person's personality more than what country they are from. But _____ get too personal too quickly. Just focus on getting the work done first. That will _____ you to build a more friendly relationship with him later.

Scenario:

Read the conversation. Write down what is wrong with what Jamie is saying. Write short suggestions for what Jamie should do to be better prepared for this call.

Zack:	Are we ready for the conference call via Zoom tomorrow afternoon?
Jamie:	Yes, we're ready. I signed up with my wife's email account. *Don't use a personal email address. Instead, use* _____
Zack:	OK. Did you check the device in the meeting room?
Jamie:	Not really. I'm sure it will be fine though. I have used it before at home, so it's OK. _____
Zack:	Alright. I think we should also take down brief notes during the call so we can refer to them after.
Jamie:	Oh, I was just planning to try to remember things in my head. _____

Scenario:

You are a member of the human resources team. Write an email to inform the employees in your company of a change in policy that will allow employees to show up an hour later for work if they work an additional hour at the end of the day. The policy is called "flextime."

Tip *Look at the checklist on p. 38 for writing tips.*

Dear colleagues,

Chapter 2 Lesson 2: Activity, pages 40–41 **Track A2-01**

Scenario:

You work for a consultancy firm, and you are meeting with THL Ltd., an important client. Listen to your client's needs and requirements and take notes. Then write an email to your manager summarizing the key points from the meeting and proposing how to move forward.

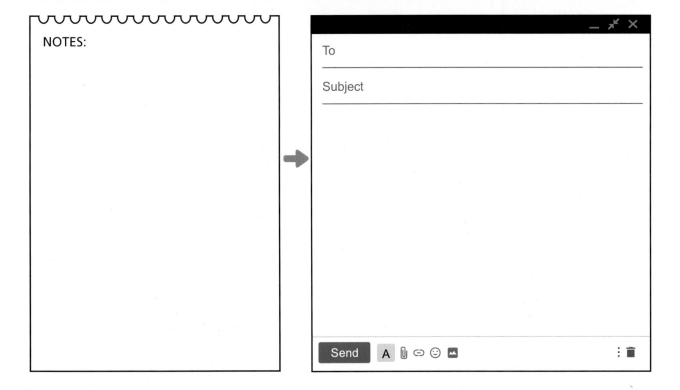

NOTES:

To

Subject

Send

Chapter 2 Lesson 3: Activity, pages 42–43

Scenario:

A colleague has asked you to check the level of formality in an email to their boss. Review the email below and make corrections to make the email more formal.

> **Tip** Look at the information on p. 42 for tips on formality.

--- ⤢ ✕

Dear

~~Hi,~~ Mr. Johansen,

I hope you are doing well.

I've attached the file you asked me to send. You also asked if we could have a meeting tomorrow afternoon. Can we postpone that meeting? I have another appointment that I cannot delay.

Please let me know when would be a good time to reschedule the meeting.

Cheers,

Stacey

Chapter 2 Lesson 4: Activity, pages 44–45 〈 Track A2-02 〉

Scenario:

Listen to your manager and take notes about various correspondences she wants you to follow up. Then use appropriate correspondence phrases from the lesson to write to the recipients.

> **Tip** Use the useful phrases on p. 44 in your answers.

Recipient	Notes	Correspondence
Client	reply to email—new billing process over $2,000	With reference to your email about billing, we have a new process for orders over $2,000.

Scenario:

Review the contract below and strengthen it by changing and improving the bolded words.

> **Tip** *Look at the contract extract on p. 47 as an example.*

Section II. Delivery of Payment

Clause A:

does not

Manufacturer **doesn't** pay Client **anything** related to taxes, duties, tariffs, or any other associated fees.

Client agrees to pay Manufacturer a total Payment of <u>US $45,000</u> upon delivery of the shipment with the following conditions met:

Condition II. A-1: Client **takes care** of full Shipment and Shipment meets delivery specifications **below**.

Condition II. A-2: **Customer** receives Shipment **about 1** month as of the execution of this contract.

All terms of Section II of this contract are legally binding and final upon the mutual agreement and signatures of both parties, the Client and the Supplier.

The provisions of this Contract shall be governed by and construed in accordance with laws of **our country**, whose courts shall be courts of competent jurisdiction.

Scenario:

You are a member of the marketing team at your company. Think of a new product or service and plan a strategy for effective online promotion. Choose a platform and decide what steps you will take to promote it.

> **Tip** *Use the flowcharts on p. 48.*

Product / Service: _____   **Marketing Platform(s):** _____

- *make regular posts*

Scenario:

Write a short report to update your colleagues about your current work. Include your name, the date, and create headings and subheadings for information about things such as budgets, schedules, progress, deadlines, challenges, etc.

Name:

Date:

In response to a request to provide an update on my current assignment, I have prepared the following report.

Scenario:

Suppose you are in charge of hiring a new member for your team at work. The first step is to post an attractive job advertisement to several recruiting sites. Write a job advertisement for your team and company.

Tip Use the checklist on p. 52.

Information about your company	_____ is a company that has been in business since _____. We do business with _____. We are hiring because _____.
Specifics about the position	
Requirements and preferences	
Expectations and benefits	
Application details	

Scenario:

Fill out the LinkedIn profile with your professional information and history.

> **Tip** *Use the checklist on p. 54.*

Name and professional contact details	*Name:* *Phone:* *Email:*
Employment history	
Alma mater	
Certifications and skills	
Professional reference	
Awards and notable accomplishments	*Outstanding Employee of the Year Award in* _____

Chapter 2 Lesson 10: Activity, pages 56–57

Scenario:

Write instructions or directions for a general audience to read on your website about something related to your company. For example, explain how to use one of your products, how to get to your office from the nearest bus station, how set up a service, etc.

Instructions: How to _____

Scenario:

Rewrite the messages and connect the two ideas within them using a coordinating conjunction (for, and, nor, but, or, yet, so).

Tip (*Use the information on p. 58.*)

1.	Many employees felt the most important thing is to highlight individual accountability. They suggested having an "Employee of the Month" award program.
	Many employees felt the most important thing is to highlight individual accountability, so they suggested having an "Employee of the Month" award program.
2.	Employees who work efficiently can be recognized through "Employee of the Month" awards. Employees who have outstanding performance can be recognized through "Employee of the Month" awards.
3.	This recommendation is the most popular idea. A list of the alternative ideas suggested by employees in the survey can be found in the latter part of the attachment.

Scenario:

Read the message that was written by a colleague. Find the mistakes, correct them, and rewrite the email.

— ⤢ ✕

hear

I was delighted to ~~here~~ that you took my advise and bought a new English dictionary.

Their very useful and will help you too practice your spelling.

I think you know that spelling is your principle weakness.

The dictionary will help you identify you're mistakes and were you must improve!

- -

I was delighted to hear

Scenario:

Listen to a phone call and take notes. Then write an email based on your notes using correct punctuation.

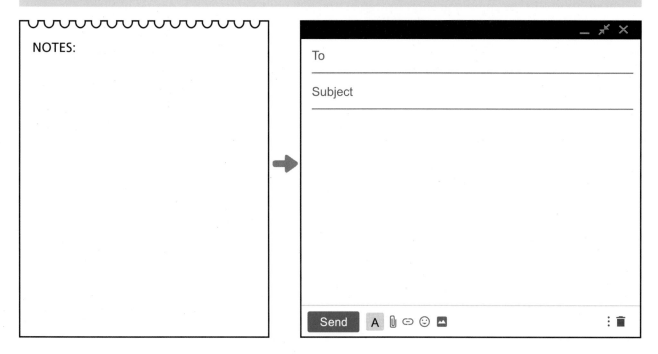

NOTES:

To

Subject

Send

Scenario:

You work for an IT company that provides a very popular instant message and email service. Until now, the messenger service did not allow users to edit or delete messages once they were sent. Due to overwhelming demand for this function, your company will allow users to edit or delete messages up to ten minutes after sending them. After ten minutes, sent messages cannot be altered. This new feature will be available next month. Write a blog post explaining this to your users.

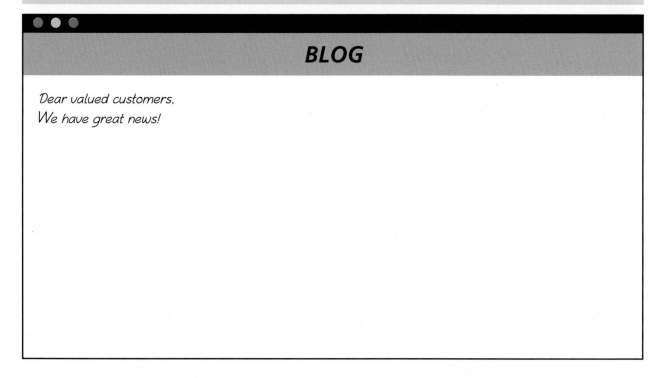

BLOG

Dear valued customers,
We have great news!

Chapter 3 Lesson 1: Activity, pages 70–71

Scenario:

You are the head of sales for a robotics firm, and you are pitching a new line of automated assembly robots to a large automobile manufacturer. Brainstorm how you plan to make a successful presentation and the communication strategies you will use to engage the potential client. Discuss with a partner and make notes in the table.

Tip | Use the checklist on p. 70.

Needs of audience	
Organization of information	
Visuals and handouts	*Use engaging visuals that demonstrate the advantages of the assembly robots, such as a video of the manufacturing process.*
Attitude, tone, and message delivery	

Chapter 3 Lesson 2: Activity, pages 72–73 Track A3-01

Scenario:

Your manager has asked you to attend an important industry conference and watch a presentation by an influential speaker. Note down the key points from the presentation so you can report back to your boss. Consider the main purpose of the presentation and the supporting information.

Identify the main aim of the presentation	a inform the audience b persuade the audience c sell something to the audience d train the audience
Key information	
Supporting information / other	

Scenario:

The head of the customer service department at a large corporation needs to organize a last-minute presentation to inform employees about a sudden change in policy. The entire department is expected to attend the presentation. Role-play a discussion between the head of customer service and the office manager to organize the location and equipment for the presentation. Choose a role and make notes in the boxes below.

Role A: Head of Customer Service You urgently need a large meeting room which can hold 35 people. Ideally you need a stage with a podium. Make sure the equipment in the room will be compatible with your laptop. Also consider audio, lighting, etc.	**Role B: Office Manager** Help the head of customer service organize a location and equipment for their meeting. Inform them that the best meeting rooms are already booked, and some of the equipment will not be available at such short notice.

Chapter 3   Lesson 4: Activity, page 76–77

Scenario:

You are a representative from the PR department of a fast-growing social media firm. You will be making a presentation at an important industry conference to introduce your platform and gain interest among investors and advertisers. Write an engaging introduction of yourself and your company in the box below.

Tip   *Use the presentation opening on p. 77 as an example.*

Good afternoon, ladies and gentlemen. Let me introduce myself. My name is...

Scenario:
Read an excerpt from a presentation and fill in the blanks with appropriate signposting language.

Tip *Review the signposting phrases on p. 78.*

Welcome to all of you, and thank you for your attention. As most of you know, I was recently made head of the future business team. Today, we'll be taking a look at how we can revolutionize our business model to remain competitive in the current climate.

_____ point I'd like to raise concerns our sales strategy. As communications technology continues to develop, it's crucial we move toward a B2C model, rather than continuing our outdated B2B focus.

_____ of my presentation. _____

_____ employee benefits and flexible working hours, we are falling way behind our competitors. Industry research has shown that more flexibility leads to a happier and more productive workforce—it's time we take note of this trend.

_____ our sales strategy. If we move toward a B2C model, we must be prepared to take care of our customers whenever they need. This means being available during evenings and weekends. _____,
a more flexible approach to working hours would benefit our employees. It can also clearly benefit our sales and customer service strategy.

_____ main thoughts I've gone through so far...

Chapter 3 Lesson 6: Activity, pages 80–81

Scenario:
The CEO of a large corporation has asked the heads of two business units to come up with new strategies to boost sales. The majority of the company's customers are in your home market, with a small number of sales overseas. Over the last year, the company has failed to grow its sales numbers. The two business unit heads have very different strategies for increasing sales. Choose a role below and try to convince the CEO to follow your strategy. Make notes in the boxes below.

Role A: Head of Business Unit 1	Role B: Head of Business Unit 2
You strongly believe that your company should focus on the domestic market. You think that it is impossible to make a product that can appeal to both the domestic and international markets. You want to focus more resources on targeting, marketing, and selling to local customers.	You strongly believe that the international market has more potential than the domestic market. You want to set a target of making 50% of all sales overseas by the end of next year. You believe that domestic sales will get smaller over the next 3–5 years.

Scenario:

Read an excerpt from a presentation on customer feedback and change the phrasing to engage the audience more effectively. Use questions and inclusive pronouns appropriately.

Tip *Review the useful phrases and inclusive language on p. 82.*

Developing a rapport with the client is important. I think some of you have probably felt lost when dealing with complaints. Right?

I'm sure many of us

~~I know I~~ have felt that way. I felt like I had to defend the product against the person making the complaint.

Now I think about it differently. I think of the complaint as an opportunity to get valuable feedback.

I don't think I can afford to ignore this kind of feedback from clients.

That's why I need to act sincerely and try to build a good relationship with my customers.

If I acknowledge what's wrong and try to fix the problem, then the customers will realize that I'm dealing with them honestly.

Chapter 3 Lesson 8: Activity, pages 84–85

Scenario:

Imagine you are giving a presentation about the financial performance of your company over the past year. Look at the graph and explain what happened in each quarter.

Tip *Use the useful language on p. 84.*

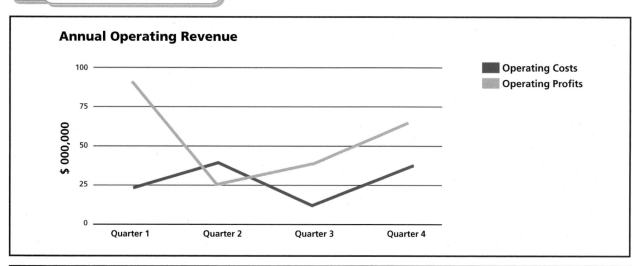

Presentation	*As you can see from this graph, in the first quarter, our operating costs*
	_____
	_____
	_____
	_____

Scenario:

You work on the product development team at a mid-sized industrial chemical company. The R&D department chief wants at least three new products developed by the end of this year. Project Team 1 is very close to completing a new product called *Agent X* and wants to start developing another called *Compound B* that it believes it can complete this year. Project Team 2 is also close to completing a new chemical product called *Trichlorothene*, but has a different view of how to get the third new product. Choose a role below and try to convince the R&D chief to follow your strategy. Make notes in the boxes below.

Tip *Use the checklist & phrases on p. 86.*

Role A: Project Team 1	Role B: Project Team 2
You believe the company should use its human resources to finish the development of *Compound B*. You also believe that Project Team 2 should join and assist your team's development of *Compound B*. While there is a possibility that you won't finish within the year, you feel the rewards outweigh the risks. You believe your plan is a better use of company resources than Project Team 2's plan.	You believe the company should use financial resources to acquire the third new chemical product from an outside company. You think human resources could be deployed more effectively. While your plan is more expensive, if you acquire the third chemical, then both Project Teams 1 and 2 can begin work on two more chemical compounds. You may then be able to finish the year with five new products.

Scenario:

You work for a cyber security company called Digiphalanx. Your colleague has sent you a software product presentation she used a few months earlier with some clients from a start-up company. You have an upcoming presentation for the same product but with clients from the financial industry. Rewrite the presentation script to be more formal, closed, and detached.

Tip *Review the useful phrases on p. 88.*

Thanks for being here today, everyone. Would you like to hear an interesting statistic before we get started? Did you know that over 87% of all companies don't have adequate cybersecurity measures in place? After hearing that, don't you agree that most businesses simply don't know how important it is? I think we can all agree that's just a catastrophe! We'll look at that in a moment, but first, let me give you a detailed history of our company and our past achievements.

On behalf of Digiphalanx, I'd like to thank you all for being here today.

Scenario:

You work for a consulting firm that helps companies improve HR and PR both internally and externally. You need to write the ending of an upcoming presentation. Review the main ideas of the presentation below and write an ending to the presentation.

Tip *Use the useful language on p. 90.*

Presentation Main Ideas

- Results aren't everything. Human relationships are an important part of work.
- You work better with people you have a good relationship with: good relationships = better results.
- To have good relationships with clients, colleagues, etc., you must have empathy.
- "Empathy" means recognizing and appreciating the value each person has, whether big or small.

Signaling the end
- *So, we're approaching the end of our talk here today.*

Summarizing the main ideas
-

Concluding
-

Final recommendation
-

Support
-

Closing
-

Inviting questions
-

Scenario:

Imagine you are a salesperson at a pharmaceutical company. You've just finished a presentation introducing the newest product offerings from your company. Listen to a series of questions from the audience and write them down. Then think of the best phrases to handle them.

Tip *Use the useful language on p. 92.*

Questions	1. 2. 3.
Responses	1. 2. 3.

Scenario:

Your colleague is preparing to give a presentation to some strict, serious, and conservative clients from another culture. Your boss has asked you to write an email with suggestions and directions for your colleague about what to wear, how to behave, and what communication and social factors to consider.

Tip Use the database on p. 94.

Hello, _____.

So I hear you have a big presentation coming up with some pretty conservative clients. The boss asked me to email you with a few tips. Here's what I suggest.

Scenario:

Imagine you work for the HR department. Due to the recent decision by your company to aggressively expand your overseas business, your team needs to train employees on how to give successful presentations. Prepare training materials which list the most important points to consider for giving a successful presentation.

Tip Use the dos and don'ts on p. 96.

Preparation: Make sure you have identified a clear purpose and goal, as well as the type of presentation you want to give.

ANSWER KEY

CHAPTER 01 English for Calls

01 What Makes a Good Call? p.7
DIALOG
device / connection / result / positive
VOCABULARY
1. style
2. suggest
3. speak
4. smart
5. room
PRACTICE
1. a 2. d 3. b 4. a 5. b

02 Making a Video Call p.9
DIALOG
account / tools / via / participants
VOCABULARY
1. b 2. a 3. e 4. c 5. d
PRACTICE
1. properly
2. chat
3. join
4. invitation
5. mute

03 Getting Through p.11
DIALOG
representative / behalf / assist / take down
VOCABULARY
1. apologize
2. hang up
3. automated
4. urgent
5. out
PRACTICE
1. b 2. d 3. c 4. a 5. e

04 Opening a Call p.13
DIALOG
advance / simplify / inquiries / FYI
VOCABULARY
1. a 2. c 3. d 4. b 5. d
PRACTICE
1. FYI 2. IMO 3. i.e. 4. doc 5. e.g.

05 Messages p.15
DIALOG
reschedule / O as in Ox / inform / corporate
VOCABULARY
1. Date
2. Address
3. reschedule
4. Action, return
PRACTICE
1. a 2. d 3. c 4. e 5. b

06 Structuring a Call p.17
DIALOG
arrange / put a pin in that / leave it to / follow up
VOCABULARY
1. d 2. a 3. e 4. c 5. b
PRACTICE
1. structuring
2. stating the purpose
3. setting action items
4. confirming
5. delaying

07 Transferring Information p.19
DIALOG
Pardon / miscommunication / read this back / exactly
VOCABULARY
1. catch
2. follow
3. respond
4. accurate
5. critical
PRACTICE
1. d 2. b 3. e 4. c 5. a

08 Communication Difficulties p.21
DIALOG
hardly / hear me now / battery / wrong
VOCABULARY
1. signal
2. speak up
3. line
4. right
5. noisy
PRACTICE
1. b 2. a 3. d 4. c 5. a

09 Calling Back p.23
DIALOG
assistant / actually / another time / journey
VOCABULARY
1. d 2. a 3. b 4. c 5. e
PRACTICE
1. insisting
2. offering an excuse
3. calling back
4. thanking
5. offering / requesting a callback

10 Making Appointments p.25
DIALOG
come up / reservation / ideal / in a few
VOCABULARY
1. e 2. b 3. c 4. a 5. d
PRACTICE
move up / change / set / reception / free

11 Complaints `p.27`

DIALOG
was made / complaint / clerical
/ as soon as possible

VOCABULARY
1. repair
2. damage
3. blame
4. attend to
5. accept

PRACTICE
1. complain → complaint
2. maked → made
3. explained → explain
4. sorry → apologize
5. sure → assure

12 Closing a Call `p.29`

DIALOG
run through / Alternatively / cooperation
/ Alright

VOCABULARY
1. run
2. slowly
3. summary
4. difficult
5. ignore

PRACTICE
1. b   2. d   3. b   4. a   5. c

13 Calls in Different Cultures `p.31`

DIALOG
respect / Mr. / safer / guarantee

VOCABULARY
1. b   2. a   3. e   4. c   5. d

PRACTICE
1. directness
2. Ms.
3. concisely
4. interrupt
5. humor

14 Business Tips for Calls `p.33`

DIALOG
via / host / assure / follow up

VOCABULARY
1. brief
2. abruptly
3. greet
4. schedule
5. purpose

PRACTICE
1. tools
2. result
3. appropriate
4. participants
5. clarify

Case Study 01 `p.34`

Part B

Sample answer
- They tend to think of time as an unlimited resource.
- Having family or personal ties is often important for business relationships.
- Respecting hierarchy is seen as extremely important.
- Speaking too directly is seen as rude
- Colleagues avoid criticizing one another in public to save 'face.'

Part C

Sample answer

How important is punctuality?
Staff: Time is seen as an unlimited resource.
Customers: Time is seen as a scarce resource.

How is directness viewed?
Staff: Directness is seen as rude.
Customers: Directness is seen as important when trying to solve a problem.

Is silence acceptable?
Staff: Short silences are not seen negatively.
Customers: Silences can be frustrating.

Are interruptions acceptable?
Staff: Interruptions are seen negatively. People usually wait for others to finish talking.
Customers: Interruptions are seen as rude.

What level of formality is best?
Staff: Being formal is seen as very important, especially when dealing with a customer or older colleague.
Customers: Politeness is seen as more important than formality.

Part D

Sample answer

Punctuality & time:
- Work quickly. Apologize if something takes time. Offer to call back if it takes longer than 1 minute
- Don't keep the customer waiting in silence for more than 10 seconds.

Level of formality:
- Keep a friendly and respectful attitude and tone. Refer to the customer as 'sir' or 'madam.'
- Ask 'How are you today?' but do not make extended small talk or ask personal questions that are unrelated to the service the customer requires.

Directness, interruptions, & silence:
- Answer questions politely, but directly. If a request is not possible then say 'I'm sorry, sir/madam, unfortunately we're not able to...'
- Don't interrupt the customer while they are speaking. Let them finish before asking further questions or making comments.

Part E

Sample answer

Customer Service Representative:
Good morning, this is Geet speaking. How may I help you today?

Customer:
I'm calling because I'm having problems with the RemMan platform. I paid for the team package, but it's not allowing me to add new users.

Customer Service Representative:
I apologize for any inconvenience caused, sir. Could I please have a few details so we can check your account? Please give me your full name and email address.

Customer:
OK. It's Fred Hampton, and my email address is fred.hampton@larksbrooke.com.

Customer Service Representative:
Thank you, sir. I'm just checking your account and there seems to be a software issue.

Customer:
Can you do something about it?

Customer Service Representative:
I'll have one of our engineers attend to it immediately. You will receive an email within 30 minutes with the status.

Customer:
Thank you. Goodbye.

01 Successful Writing `p.39`

DIALOG

jargon / long and short of it / relevant / specifically

VOCABULARY

1. a   2. d   3. c   4. a   5. b

PRACTICE

1. contents   2. related
3. punctuation   4. unnecessary
5. sidetracked

02 Organizing Information `p.41`

DIALOG

report / pyramid / with / practical

VOCABULARY

1. d   2. a   3. e   4. c   5. b

PRACTICE

1. promotional   2. stages
3. chronology   4. conclusion
5. outline

03 Business Emails `p.43`

EMAIL

Can / attachment / confidential / cc

VOCABULARY

1. emphasis   2. salutation
3. forward   4. consistent
5. adequate

PRACTICE

1. Dear Susan,   2. I am
3. Could you please 4. I would
5. Best regards,

04 Correspondence Phrases `p.45`

EMAIL

grateful / inconvenience / delighted / We look forward to

VOCABULARY

1. inquire   2. far
3. process   4. lowly
5. help

PRACTICE

1. regret   2. manufacturing
3. refund   4. experience
5. inquire

05 Contracts & MOUs `p.47`

CONTRACT

Client / takes custody / contract / parties

VOCABULARY

1. d　2. b　3. c　4. e　5. a

PRACTICE

1. c　2. a　3. b　4. d　5. e

06 Promotional Materials `p.49`

POST

customers / channel / audience / feedback

VOCABULARY

1. d　2. b　3. a　4. d　5. c

PRACTICE

1. We thank our customers for their feedback.
2. Most of the people who had signed up viewed the live stream.
3. Our followers wrote many comments.
4. You left valuable feedback.
5. Our team planned three more videos.

07 Business Reports `p.51`

SUMMARY

investigation / recommendations / headings / sub-

VOCABULARY

1. title　2. justify
3. budget　4. figures
5. update

PRACTICE

1. b　2. a　3. e　4. d　5. c

08 Job Openings `p.53`

JOB AD

scaling / growth / competitive salary / hired

VOCABULARY

1. present　2. go
3. functional　4. natural
5. requirement

PRACTICE

1. c　2. a　3. b　4. d　5. c

09 Cover Letters & Résumés `p.55`

DIALOG

irrelevant / alma mater / references / template

VOCABULARY

1. b　2. d　3. e　4. a　5. c

PRACTICE

1. employer　2. alma mater
3. accomplishments　4. competencies
5. distinguish

10 Technical Language `p.57`

INSTRUCTIONS

operating / should / perform / code

VOCABULARY

1. d　2. a　3. c　4. e　5. b

PRACTICE

1. c　2. a　3. d　4. b　5. a

11 Connecting Words `p.59`

EMAIL

highlight / efficiently / bring about / aforementioned

VOCABULARY

1. c　2. b　3. d　4. a　5. e

PRACTICE

1. alternative　2. Consequently
3. latter　4. partial
5. mentioning

12 Grammar & Spelling Check `p.61`

DIALOG

reputation / rely on / nonessential / advice

VOCABULARY

1. analyze　2. mitigate
3. remove　4. rely on
5. avoid

PRACTICE

1. correctly　2. has been
3. are　4. arrived
5. be

13 Punctuation `p.63`

DIALOG

punctuated / introductory / clause / at symbol

VOCABULARY

1. ask　2. careful
3. quickly　4. promise
5. reported

PRACTICE

1. d　2. a　3. e　4. b　5. c

14 Business Tips for Writing `p.65`

DIALOG

drafted / logically / strengthen / coordinated

VOCABULARY

1. b　2. e　3. a　4. d　5. c

PRACTICE

1. terminology　2. preparation
3. assume　4. jargon
5. appropriate

Part C

Sample answer

Pros
- can report new things that happen during the day
- can help the manager understand and evaluate employees' work

Both
- emails are private: you can discuss issues privately with the boss, but it also means colleagues can't help each other with those problems
- takes around 30 minutes every day: doesn't take too long, but time could be used for other things

Cons
- most information is the same as discussed in morning meeting
- employees never get any feedback

Part D

Sample answer

Good afternoon, Craig,

As discussed, I have reviewed the opinions about progress reports on the internal message board and come up with some conclusions and recommendations.

First of all, I'd like to summarize the opinions given in support of keeping or eliminating the current system.

Keep the current system:
- allows team members to update you with new things that have happened throughout the day
- allows team members to inform you about problems and concerns privately

Eliminate the current system:
- progress reports are unnecessary because project status is discussed in the daily morning meetings
- because emails are not public, team members cannot advise each other on arising issues

Having reviewed these opinions, I believe we can improve the system to make it more efficient. I suggest we create a public document where employees can list their current tasks and update task status at the end of each day. Any issues or delays can then be discussed openly in the morning meeting the following day.

However, I think it's also important that team members have the opportunity to speak to you privately if they have any concerns they don't want to share with the entire team.

Please let me know if you'd like any further information.

Best,

CHAPTER 03 English for Presentations

01 What Makes a Good Presentation? p.71
DIALOG
complexity / allotted / visuals / distracting

VOCABULARY
1. rhythm	2. promote
3. strategically	4. maximum
5. nervous	

PRACTICE
1. b	2. a	3. c	4. e	5. d

02 Presentation Types p.73
DIALOG
purchase / persuade / training / My goal is to

VOCABULARY
1. advertisement	2. product
3. see	4. discuss
5. unclear	

PRACTICE
1. a	2. d	3. b	4. c	5. c

03 Equipment & Environment p.75
DIALOG
podium / Perfect / Could you / temperature

VOCABULARY
1. b	2. d	3. a	4. d	5. c

PRACTICE
1. b	2. e	3. a	4. d	5. c

04 Starting a Presentation p.77
MONOLOG
obtain / comprehend / market / fact

VOCABULARY
1. c	2. e	3. a	4. d	5. b

PRACTICE
1. begin	2. topic
3. split	4. take a look at
5. examine	

05 Signposting p.79
MONOLOG
As I will explain to you in a moment / final / turn to / thoughts

VOCABULARY
1. however	2. moreover
3. postpone	4. move
5. as you know	

PRACTICE
1. b	2. d	3. e	4. c	5. a

06 Highlighting & Emphasizing `p.81`

MONOLOG
contrast / rather / reiterate / achieve

VOCABULARY
1. e   2. a   3. b   4. d   5. c

PRACTICE
1. emphasize   2. improvements
3. remarkable   4. options
5. absolute

07 Engaging Your Audience `p.83`

DIALOG
rapport / diplomatic / us / honestly

VOCABULARY
1. b   2. d   3. e   4. a   5. c

PRACTICE
1. d   2. e   3. a   4. c   5. b

08 Visuals `p.85`

MONOLOG
graph / volatility / significant / stable

VOCABULARY
1. b   2. c   3. a   4. e   5. d

PRACTICE
1. a   2. c   3. e   4. d   5. b

09 Body Language & Persuasion `p.87`

DIALOG
proposal / risky / posture / absolute must

VOCABULARY
1. b   2. c   3. e   4. a   5. d

PRACTICE
1. a   2. a   3. c   4. b   5. d

10 Communication Styles `p.89`

MONOLOG
overstate / catastrophe / just / perceive

VOCABULARY
1. d   2. a   3. b   4. e   5. c

PRACTICE
1. emotionally   2. worry
3. systematic   4. Naturally
5. agree

11 Closing a Presentation `p.91`

MONOLOG
approaching / forge / appoint / famously said

VOCABULARY
1. advice   2. meet
3. questionable   4. differently
5. hear

PRACTICE
1. overseas   2. partnerships
3. demand   4. attentively
5. recommend

12 Handling Questions `p.93`

DIALOG
allow / beyond / complex / let me ask you

VOCABULARY
1. liberty   2. glad
3. difficult   4. correctly
5. fully

PRACTICE
1. another → other
2. making → make
3. certainly → certain
4. fare → fair
5. mention → mentioned

13 Presentations in Different Cultures `p.95`

DIALOG
consider / contribute / in some Asian cultures / rigid

VOCABULARY
1. c   2. a   3. b   4. e   5. d

PRACTICE
1. d   2. a   3. c   4. b   5. e

14 Business Tips for Presenting `p.97`

DIALOG
So that concludes / mannerisms / point / talk

VOCABULARY
1. e   2. c   3. b   4. d   5. a

PRACTICE
1. covers   2. talk
3. recommend   4. idea
5. summarizing

Case Study 03 `p.98`

Part B
Sample answer

Internal
- rising operating costs
- falling profits
- staff shortages

External
- global recession
- changes to government regulation
- increasing transportation costs

Reward Potential
- overseas growth potential
- increase value of stocks and shares
- reduction / mitigation of risk through market diversification

Part C

Presentation type
- Persuade the audience

Main idea
- Our company should have a balanced risk management portfolio for the coming year.

Supporting Points
- The global economic situation makes the benefit of overseas expansion uncertain.
- Government regulation in the domestic and international market means we should invest in new ways of delivering our current products rather than developing new products.
- Keeping cash in reserve while pushing current products will protect against further economic crises while making the most of our current IP.

Part D

1. Good morning, everybody.

   As most of you know, starting last month I became the new CFO.

   Today, we'll be taking a look at our risk management strategy for the coming year.

   Today's talk is particularly pertinent given the current condition of the global economy.

2. I've divided today's presentation into three sections.

   First, we'll examine the challenges our business is currently facing. Second, we'll discuss how we can protect ourselves in the current economic climate. Third, we'll talk about how we can actually increase our market share.

   OK, let's get started.

3. I'd like to begin by asking you a question. How can we boost our sales during a recession using only existing products?

Activity File

Chapter 1 Lesson 1: Activity `p.100`

Sample answer

Hi, Joe,

I would like you to help prepare for tomorrow's conference call. Please do the following tasks:
- Prepare all the documents and information we need for the discussion.
- Email Pedro to confirm the time of the call.
- Check the connection, display, and settings on the laptop we'll use for the call.

Let me know if you have any questions.

Thanks,

Chapter 1 Lesson 2: Activity `p.100`

Sample answer
- Be sure to use a professional, secure email address: not a private one.
- Send participants a group message to confirm their attendance in advance of the call.
- Create, test, and send the call link to all participants in advance of the meeting.
- Launch the calling program a few minutes before the call and admit participants promptly.
- Ask participants to mute while others are talking and use the chat function to send important documents.

Chapter 1 Lesson 3: Activity `p.101`

Sample answer
Role A
- Good morning, KS Games. My name is Toshinari.
- What is your call in regard to?
- Please hold while I check her availability for you.
- I'm sorry, but I'm afraid Tanya is out on business just now.

Role B
- Good morning. My name is Liam.
- I would like to speak to the head of the marketing team. I'm looking to help advertise your new game.
- Sure, thank you.
- Could you deliver a message for me?

Chapter 1 Lesson 4: Activity `p.101`

Sample answer

Sales Team Head:

I would like to know more about the changes to the customer billing process.

Accounting:

Sure, I'll send you a doc with all that information now.

Sales Team Head:

Great. Could you tell me about the policy for shipping fees? Will the customer or the company pay for international and domestic shipping?

Accounting:

The company will pay for all domestic shipping fees, but we will only pay 50% toward international shipping.

Chapter 1 Lesson 5: Activity `p.102`

Sample answer

• Rosa from Pacifica Health Services Limited.
• Reschedule conference call with Bill
• 17th, 10:15 a.m.
• 808–730–2024

Chapter 1 Lesson 6: Activity `p.102`

Sample answer

Jack: I'm calling to discuss two things. First, I need to ask about billing for an order. Second, I'd like to request information about a new product.

Fred: Sorry, I'm not able to deal with those items. Would it be alright if we put a pin in that until my manager returns from a business trip?

Jack: Alright, no problem. Should I call back at a later date or leave a message?

Fred: She will be back on the 15th. Please call back then and she'll be happy to help you.

Jack: Great, thank you for that.

Fred: Is there anything else?

Jack: No, that's everything. Thank you.

Chapter 1 Lesson 7: Activity `p.103`

Sample answer

A: Could you give Sam a message for me when he gets in? Are you ready?

B: Yes, please go ahead.

A: His sister Myra is arriving tonight, but I'm busy at work.

B: Pardon? Could you **spell the name, please**?

A: That's -M as in **Mom**, -Y as in **Yarn**, -R as in **Ram**, -A as in **Apple**.

B: She's on the 7:50 flight from Denver.

A: Sorry, **but the connection seems to be** breaking up. **Did you say** 7:15?

B: No, fifty. Five zero. From Denver. **It's** critical **Sam gets the** message.

A: Just to make sure there are not any **mistakes**, can you **read that back** to me, please?

Chapter 1 Lesson 8: Activity `p.103`

Sample answer

1. c

You keep cutting out. Do you have a bad connection?

2. d

Sorry, there's no one here by that name. I think you have the wrong number.

Chapter 1 Lesson 9: Activity `p.104`

Sample answer

• Hello, this is Steve of Nature Market.
• I got your message, so I'm returning your call.
• Thank you for letting me get back to you.
• With respect to what you asked me before, I would like to inform you that your order has been shipped successfully. I will send an invoice for that over to you now.

Chapter 1 Lesson 10: Activity `p.104`

Sample answer

A: So, we are supposed to have that lunch meeting today. What is your schedule like?

B: I will have a conference call until 11:30. So after that is more convenient for me.

A: Sorry, I have an international client call from 11 a.m. to 1 p.m. Are you free at around 1:15?

B: I'm afraid I'll be in a meeting with online advertisers till 4 p.m.

A: I see. It seems difficult to arrange a lunch meeting today, then.

B: Could we possibly move our meeting to tomorrow instead of today?

A: That sounds great.

Chapter 1 Lesson 11: Activity p.105

Sample answer

A: Hello, this is TYJ Sports Equipment. I'm a customer service representative, and my name is Miranda. How can I assist you today?

B: Hello, this is HS Sports Store. I'm calling to make a complaint. I believe a mistake has been made with an order we made.

A: Could you explain exactly what the issue is?

B: I ordered 300 soccer balls a week ago, but only 30 balls have arrived.

A: I'm very sorry. It seems there has been a clerical error. Our records show that you ordered 30 balls, not 300.

B: Well, I definitely remember ordering 300. Can you do something about it?

A: I apologize for any inconvenience caused. I'll deal with it right away.

B: OK, thank you. Please get those to me as soon as possible.

Chapter 1 Lesson 12: Activity p.105

Sample answer

1. a

Sure, tomorrow morning will work for me. Let's say 11:30?

2. c

Definitely. I'm very grateful for your cooperation on that point. And yes, I'll be there to collect you from the airport. See you soon. Goodbye.

Chapter 1 Lesson 13: Activity p.106

Sample answer

A: I'm a little worried about calling Mr. Svenson in Sweden. I don't know anything about Swedish culture. Do you have any suggestions?

B: Well, I've heard that they like **punctuality**, so make sure to be on time.

A: Right. Actually, now that you mention it, I do remember hearing that before too. What about directness? A lot of Americans tend to be very direct, but some other cultures find that a little rude or aggressive.

B: Hmm. Well, I think that directness is probably a similarity they have with us. I think they **might not mind** that because they think it shows honesty.

A: Alright. Well, I want to make a good impression and get a good result. Gaining his trust is important, but what about using **humor**? Is it OK to make jokes?

B: Well, I guess that depends on each person's personality more than what country they are from. But **it's safer not to** get too personal too quickly. Just focus on getting the work done first. That will **enable** you to build a more friendly relationship with him later.

Chapter 1 Lesson 14: Activity p.106

Sample answer

- Don't use a personal email address. Instead, use a corporate one.
- Don't forget to check the device's status in advance so that you can prevent any problems that could occur during the conference.
- Make sure to take brief notes so that you can review the notes after the call if you need to.

Chapter 2 Lesson 1: Activity p.107

Sample answer

Dear colleagues,

I'm excited to reveal the details of our new flextime policy.

As many of you know, management has been working hard to find ways not only to increase productivity but also to improve employee satisfaction.

We have decided to make working hours more flexible so you can all build work schedules that suit you.

From the beginning of next month, employees can choose one of three shifts:
- 8 a.m. to 4 p.m.
- 9 a.m. to 5 p.m.
- 10 a.m. to 6 p.m.

Please inform your team heads about your choice before the end of the week.

Have a great day.

Chapter 2 Lesson 2: Activity p.107

Sample answer

Good morning, Sahid,

The meeting this morning with THL Ltd. was very successful. They are very happy with the work we have done over the past few years.

The client has two requirements for the coming year. First, they need help to scale up their supply chain to meet growing demand. Second, they have asked us to look into a sales and distribution channel in South America for a planned expansion there.

The client requires plans for these two points by the beginning of next month. I suggest we create two teams so we can make recommendations for both requests quickly and effectively.

Please let me know if you need any further information.

Regards,

Sample answer

~~*Dear*~~
Hi, Mr. Johansen,
I hope you are doing well.
I have
~~**I've**~~ attached the file you asked me to send. You also asked if we could have a meeting

Could we please
tomorrow afternoon. ~~**Can we**~~ postpone that meeting? I have another appointment that I cannot delay.
Please let me know when would be a good time to reschedule the meeting.
Best Regards,
~~**Cheers**~~,
Stacey Anderson

Sample answer
Client:
- With reference to your email about the billing, we have a new process for orders over $2,000.

Distribution Partner in Chile:
- We regret to inform you that our next shipment to you will be delayed by two weeks. We apologize for any inconvenience this causes.

Parts Supplier:
- Could you please double the size of our next delivery?

Head Office:
- I'm just writing to inform you about the following three issues...

Sample answer
does not   *any expenses*
Manufacturer ~~**doesn't**~~ pay Client ~~**anything**~~ related to taxes, duties, tariffs, or any other associated fees.

takes custody
Condition II. A-1: Client ~~**takes care**~~ of full Shipment and Shipment meets delivery
in Appendix B
specifications ~~**below**~~.

Client
Condition II. A-2: ~~**Customer**~~ receives
no later than 1
Shipment ~~**about 1**~~ month as of the execution of this contract.

The provisions of this Contract shall be governed by and construed in accordance
the United States of America
with laws of ~~**our country**~~, whose courts shall be courts of competent jurisdiction.

Sample answer
Product / Service: Online language classes
Platform(s): Instagram, YouTube, TikTok
- advertise product on multiple social media popular with Gen Z and Millennials
- post engaging clips of lessons with top teachers
- utilize user data to retarget engaged users on multiple platforms
- re-edit videos and create fresh content for each platform, i.e.
  - full sample lessons live on YouTube
  - short clips of fun and engaging language activities for Instagram and TikTok

Sample answer
Name: Henry Yun
Date: Sep 12th
In response to a request to provide an update on my current assignment, I have prepared the following report.

Progress:
The project is moving ahead roughly as scheduled. We may need an extra day to complete phase two. However, we can catch up by reducing the time we spend on phrase three.

Budget:
We are currently under budget. This means we should be able to save 10% on costs overall.

Challenges:
We have had a few issues with the outsourced workers we've been using for this project. Nevertheless, this shouldn't affect the overall quality of our work.

Sample answer
- HomeSmartz is a company that has been in business since 2015. We do business with residential property developers who want to integrate smart technology into the homes they offer. We are hiring because we need a driven sales professional to help take our business to the next level.
- As a member of the sales team, you'll be expected to take on and service an existing portfolio of clients and develop new business.
- We are looking for a sales professional with up to ten years' experience. Experience in the real estate or IoT technology industries is desirable, but not required.
- If you come and work for us, you can expect a competitive salary and benefits package. Our top salespeople can also expect to receive generous annual bonuses.
- Be sure to click the link below to fill out our online application form.

Sample answer
Name: Justin Case
Phone: 080 7782 6579
Email: justin.case@gmail.com

Employment History:
2010–2020 Restate
Sales Executive—servicing a portfolio of clients and developing new business

Alma Mater:
2006–2010 University of Queensland
Major: Real Estate Management GPA: 4.0

Certifications & Skills:
2017 Certified International Property Specialist

Professional Reference:
Haruto Sato,
Head of Sales, Restate
haruto.sato@restate.com

Awards & Notable Accomplishments:
Outstanding Employee of the Year Award in 2018

Instructions: How to use our app
Scan the QR code above and download our app from Google Play or the App Store.

Open the app and create a username and password. Alternatively, you can sign in using your social media profile.

The app contains a number of useful features. Browse the menu to find the tool you are looking for.

In order to help us keep growing and improving our app, please visit the *Thoughts?* tab and let us know about your experience.

Sample answer
1. Many employees felt the most important thing is to highlight individual accountability, **so** they suggested having an "Employee of the Month" award program.

2. Employees who work efficiently **and** have outstanding performance can be recognized through "Employee of the Month" awards.

3. This recommendation is the most popular idea, **but** a list of the alternative ideas suggested by employees in the survey can be found in the latter part of the attachment.

Sample answer
I was delighted to **here** *(hear)* that you took my **advise** *(advice)* and bought a new English dictionary. **Their** *(They're)* very useful and will help you **too** *(to)* practice your spelling.

I think you know that spelling is your **principle** *(principal)* weakness.

The dictionary will help you identify **you're** *(your)* mistakes and **were** *(where)* you must improve!

Sample answer
To: Yoona Kim
Subject: Trip Objectives

Hi, Yoona,

Lawrence called and he wants me to let you know about a few items he'd like you to deal with while you're on your trip:
• Move ahead with the Moldova shipment.
• Contact a European marketing company.
• Make arrangements for a trip to London next week.
• Contact some African distributors.
• Meet Justin Crawford (one of Lawrence's business partners) at the expo and collect the merchandise.

Lawrence is currently on a flight to Mexico, so he'll be out of contact for the next 11 hours or so. Please let me know if you need any further information or assistance.

Best,
Alfie

Sample answer
Dear valued customers,

We have great news! Today we're announcing the release of our long-awaited "delete message" function. For too long, sending a message to the wrong person accidentally has led to misunderstandings, embarrassment, and even arguments. This new feature will change all that.

If you send a message on our app that you are unhappy with, you now have ten minutes to delete or edit it.

Thank you all for your feedback over the last year. Without you, we wouldn't have been able to continue growing and improving our product.

Sample answer

Needs of Audience:
The audience are manufacturing specialists with lots of experience in factory-related technology. The presentation needs to focus on why our assembly robots are better than the existing system. Avoid talking about details of the manufacturing process which they may already know.

Organization of Information:
The selling points of our assembly robots—why they will make the factory safer, more efficient, and profitable—should be introduced immediately at the beginning of the presentation.

Visuals & Handouts:
Use engaging visuals that demonstrate the advantages of the assembly robots, such as a video of the manufacturing process.

Attitude, Tone & Message Delivery:
Be confident and make eye contact with the factory manager while making the presentation. Use hand gestures to help illustrate the manufacturing process.

Chapter 3 Lesson 2: Activity `p.114`

Sample answer

Main aim of the presentation:
c sell something to the audience

Key information:
Remote working is an important trend. Dacia Inc.'s RemMan platform can help us improve our task monitoring of remote workers.

Supporting information / other:
Task achievement is a more important metric than how busy people look. Dacia's platform can help us measure this metric.

Chapter 3 Lesson 3: Activity `p.115`

Sample answer

A: Morning, Gary. I'm hoping you can help me with something.

B: Sure, what do you need?

A: I need to use a meeting room to give a presentation to my department. Can you get me a large room for this afternoon? It needs to fit 35 people.

B: This afternoon? That could be difficult. The main meeting rooms are already booked by other teams. I can get you the space in the basement. What equipment do you need?

A: I want to use my laptop to show a presentation and some video. So I need a projector compatible with my laptop and a good audio system. Would it also be possible to dim the lights?

B: I don't think the basement room will be suitable for you, then. Can we move the meeting to tomorrow? I can get you the room with the podium and stage.

A: OK, let's do that then. Thanks, Gary.

Chapter 3 Lesson 4: Activity `p.115`

Sample answer

Good afternoon, ladies and gentlemen. Let me introduce myself. My name is Dmitry Sokolov and I'm here to talk to you about Gabber.

Today, we'll be taking a look at how Gabber has revolutionized the world of social media, and what that means for you.

I've divided today's presentation into three sections. First, I'll show you what makes Gabber so different from conventional social media platforms. Second, we'll discuss how Gabber will change the world of advertising for the better. And third, we'll look at what this all means for you.

Alright, let's begin by looking at an important statistic. Eighty percent of regular social media users feel that advertising negatively affects their social media experience. That means you are only…

Chapter 3 Lesson 5: Activity `p.116`

Sample answer

Welcome to all of you, and thank you for your attention. As most of you know, I was recently made head of the future business team. Today, we'll be taking a look at how we can revolutionize our business model to remain competitive in the current climate.

The first point I'd like to raise concerns our sales strategy. As communications technology continues to develop, it's crucial we move toward a B2C model, rather than continuing our outdated B2B focus.

Let's now turn to the next part of my presentation. **With respect to** employee benefits and flexible working hours, we are falling way behind our competitors. Industry research has shown that more flexibility leads to a happier and more productive workforce—it's time we take note of this trend.

Let me now return to our sales strategy. If we move toward a B2C model, we must be prepared to take care of our customers whenever they need. This means being available during evenings and weekends. **As I mentioned earlier**, a more flexible approach to working hours would benefit our employees. It can also clearly benefit our sales and customer service strategy.

Alright, I'd like to sum up the main thoughts I've gone through so far…

Sample answer

Head of Business Unit 1:

As you know, we have been struggling to grow sales this year. We need to do something, and we need to do it now. The truth is that we can't make a product that will please both our domestic customers and international customers. Their needs and tastes are very different. The domestic market is where nearly all of our sales are made. We know we can be successful here.

To put it simply, we need to invest less in trying to get into the global market, and focus more resources domestically.

Head of Business Unit 2:

It's critical to understand that we can't grow any further in the domestic market. We've sold as much as we can here. The truth is that domestic sales are likely to actually shrink over the next 3-5 years. We need to find new customers in new markets. What I'd like to do is make a big push internationally. I think we can make 50% of our sales in the global market by the end of next year if we start investing more in targeting and marketing to overseas consumers.

Sample answer

Developing a rapport with the client is important. I think some of you have probably felt lost when dealing with complaints. Right?

I'm sure many of us ~~I know I~~ have felt that way. *We felt like we had* ~~I felt like I had~~ to defend the product against the person making the complaint.

Now, I think about it differently. I think of the complaint as an opportunity to get valuable feedback.

Can we afford to ignore feedback from clients?
~~I don't think I can afford to ignore this kind of feedback from clients~~.

we
That's why ~~I~~ need to act sincerely and try to
our
build a good relationship with ~~my~~ customers.
we
If ~~I~~ acknowledge what's wrong and try to fix the problem, then the customers will realize
we're
that ~~I'm~~ dealing with them honestly.

Sample answer

As you can see from this graph, in the first quarter our operating costs gradually increased, while our operating profits plummeted.

In the middle of the second quarter, operating costs began to fall again, and profits started to make a recovery.

In the third and fourth quarters, profits continued to recover. However, they did not return to their Q1 levels. Although costs sank to a low in the middle of Q3, they steadily rose again through Q4, almost reaching the previous Q2 peak.

Sample answer

Project Team 1

By the end of this quarter, we will have completed *Agent X*. We already have plans to begin developing *Compound B* next quarter. This will be a difficult product to produce, but the potential profit is huge. My suggestion is that Team 1 and Team 2 work together on *Compound B*. If we don't use all our resources to complete *Compound B*, then our competitors will likely take our market share.

Project Team 2

Our product, *Trichloromethane*, is also near completion. On the one hand, we could invest all our time in one product, as Team 1 suggests. On the other hand, we could work on two separate chemical compounds. We could also purchase a third new chemical from our partners in China. Instead of finishing the year with three products, we could have five. Our plan will require a higher budget, but it is far less risky than investing everything in *Compound B*.

Sample answer

Good afternoon, ladies and gentlemen. On behalf of Digiphalanx, I'd like to welcome you today. First, I want to share an important statistic with you. Over 87% of all companies don't have adequate cybersecurity measures in place. I believe that many businesses just don't realize quite how important it is. As I'm sure you will all agree, this is a concern.

The consequences of this will be looked at in more depth in just a moment. Let me first give you a detailed history of our company and past achievements.

Sample answer

Signaling the end

So, we're approaching the end of our talk here today.

Summarizing the main ideas

If I can briefly summarize, we've talked today about how to not only improve relationships between people in the workplace but also how to improve results.

Concluding

To conclude, I'd like to say that the only way to create strong relationships is to have empathy.

Final recommendation

It seems to me, then, that to have good relationships with clients and colleagues we must have empathy.

Support

Here are my contact details in case you want to follow up.

Closing

Thank you for listening so attentively. You've been wonderful.

Inviting questions

I'd be glad to answer any questions at this time.

Sample answer

Questions:

1. What are the differences and similarities between the chemicals the research scientists used in the first drug compared with the second?
2. Your competitor offers a similar drug to the third drug you spoke about, but they offer it at a cheaper price. How do you respond to that?
3. What kinds of new drugs are you planning to talk about next year?

Responses:

1. Unfortunately, I'm the wrong person to answer that because I'm not a research scientist. But what I can do is put you in contact with our R&D team.
2. That's a fair point. We're working on lowering our prices.
3. I'm afraid that question goes beyond the subject for today.

Sample answer

Hello, James,

So I hear you have a big presentation coming up with some pretty conservative clients. The boss asked me to email you with a few tips. Here's what I suggest:

- Remain reserved and don't show too much personality. These clients will be focused more on business than getting to know you personally.
- Don't expect the clients to speak or ask questions during the presentation. They will likely just listen and then ask any questions at the end.
- Keep the presentation precise and straightforward. Just focus on the facts.
- Fact-check your presentation. The clients will likely bring a colleague with specialist knowledge of this particular topic.
- Dress smartly and avoid putting your hands in your pockets.
- Remember to bring your business cards, and definitely don't be late.

Let me know if you have any more questions and I'll be happy to help.

Best,

Sample answer

Preparation:

Make sure you have identified a clear purpose and goal, as well as the type of presentation you want to give. Always make sure the presentation venue is up to standard—check the audio, stage, temperature, etc.

Starting:

Follow the WISE OWL process to begin your presentation effectively and use a hook to get people's attention.

Presenting:

Outline the objective of the presentation clearly and use signposting as you move between different sections. Emphasize key ideas and remember to summarize before moving to your next point.

Concluding:

Finish your presentation within the allotted time and deliver a strong conclusion. Give your recommendations and answer any questions from the audience.

MEMO